Laura Wilson, Editor and General Manager of Nitty Gritty Cookbooks, has been involved with cookbook publishing for five years. She has written two cookbooks of her own with a friend.

Laura is active in craft shows, catering and demonstrating dishes from her cookbooks, as well as selling folk art crafts. One day she would like to own a restaurant or a small bed and breakfast inn in the Gold Mine country of California.

Celebrate the 20th Anniversary of Nitty Gritty Cookbooks

- Nitty Gritty Cookbooks has sold over 8,000,000 cookbooks containing more than 6,000 mouthwatering recipes.

- The Best of Nitty Gritty features the best recipes from Nitty Gritty's current titles in print.

- Emphasis on fresh, easy to find ingredients.

- As with all Nitty Gritty Cookbooks, the recipes are easy to follow and are printed one per page, in large, easy to read type.

- For added convenience, this book is uniquely designed to take a minimum of counter space and to keep your place when pressed open.

THE BEST OF
NITTY GRITTY

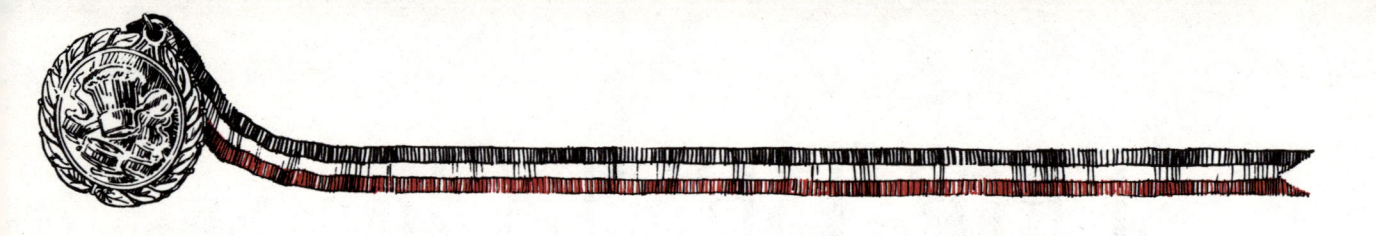

Copyright 1987
Nitty Gritty Productions
P.O. Box 2008
Benicia, CA 94510-2008

A Nitty Gritty Cookbook
Printed by Mariposa Press
Benicia, California

All rights reserved. This book or any part
thereof may not be reproduced without
the written permission of the publisher.

ISBN 0-911954-86-4

Editor: Laura Wilson
Art Director: Mike Nelson
Photographer: Glen Millward
Food Stylist: Bobbie Greenlaw

Special thanks to Margie Lear
for the china used in our cover photographs.

Table of Contents

Introduction

1987 marks the 20th anniversary of Nitty Gritty Cookbooks. The Best of Nitty Gritty is a selection compiled by myself and our authors in order to provide a special cookbook for this special year.

All of the recipes in this book are selected from Nitty Gritty Cookbooks which are still in print and are available at stores throughout the United States.

We are often asked how Nitty Gritty Cookbooks came to be. We think you will find the story to be an interesting one.

An old friend of Earl Goldman's (publisher of Nitty Gritty), Maxcy Callahan, convinced Earl that he should help her publish a Fondue cookbook. This was in late 1967. At that time fondue pots were one of the fastest selling items in housewares and gourmet shops. Earl told Maxcy that he was not interested in becoming involved in such a venture and she left.

About a month later she came back to Earl's office with a large brown envelope and said, "let's go into the conference room." They did and she emptied the contents of the envelope onto the conference table and Earl was surprised to see orders for 5,000 Fondue cookbooks from a large variety of well known retail stores. Earl agreed to provide the funds and to do the paper-

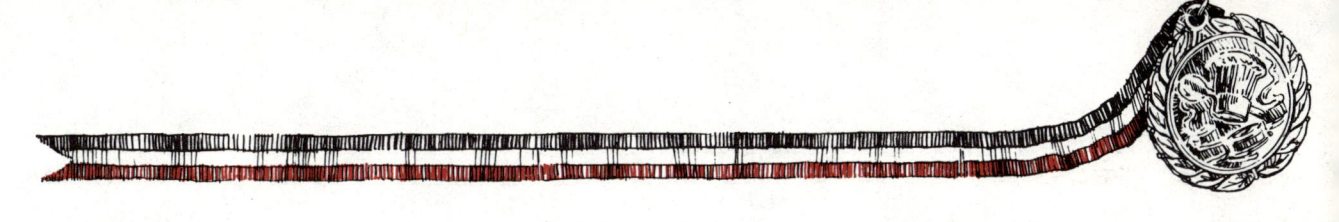

work so that the 5,000 books could be printed and sold, with the understanding that would be the end of it.

About two months went by and again Maxcy appeared in Earl's office, again with a large brown envelope filled with orders for 5,000 books. This was a shock to Earl because he couldn't understand how more than 5,000 people could ever want a Fondue cookbook. However he reluctantly agreed to go ahead and print the second batch.

True to form another two months went by and again Maxcy appeared in Earl's office, this time with a bigger brown envelope containing orders for 18,000 Fondue cookbooks. We printed and shipped those and again Maxcy appeared with orders for 20,000 additional cookbooks.

At this point Earl decided that he should try to print enough books to have an inventory for future orders instead of just printing after orders were received and we printed 40,000 cookbooks, all of which were quickly sold.

It then seemed to make sense to come out with additional books and become a true publisher.

Maxcy Callahan handled sales for Nitty Gritty Cookbooks for many years, and is today retired in Northern California. She was the inspiration and provided the marketing for our company for

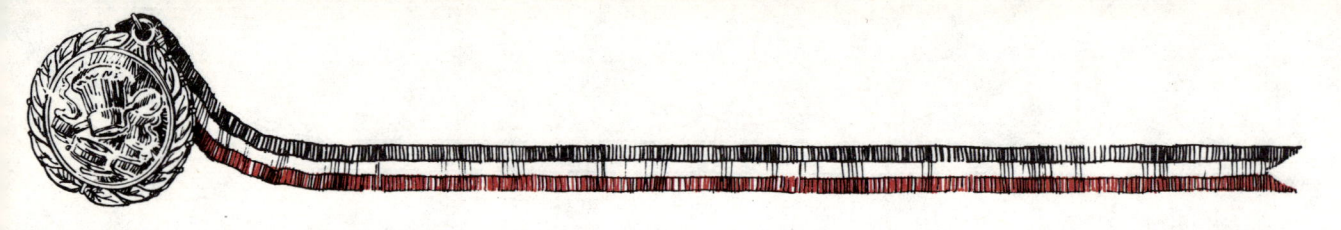

many years. Incidentally, the Fondue cookbook is still in print, and still sells many thousands of copies every year.

So it's been an interesting 20 years for us during which we have produced and sold over 8,000,000 cookbooks. Out of the 72 titles which we have published, 28 are still in print and this book along with our new Mexican cookbook brings the total to 30. We know you will enjoy using these special recipes, and if you have a moment to write us and tell us what you think of this type of book, we'd sincerely appreciate your comments.

Laura Wilson
Editor

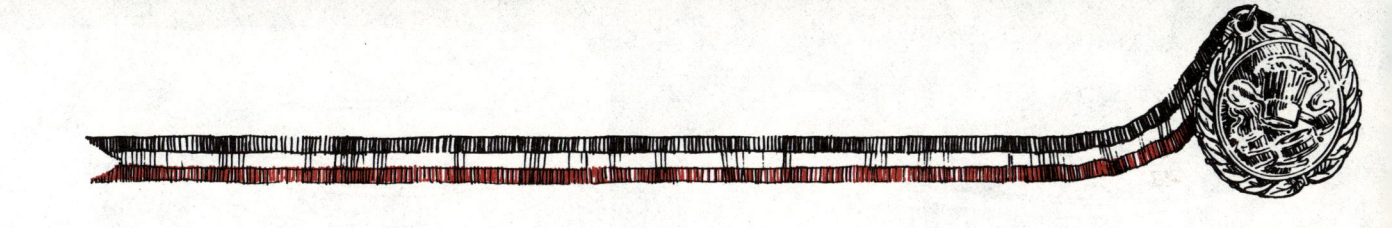

"This book is dedicated to Maxcy Callahan.
Without her perseverance
and her large brown envelopes,
Nitty Gritty would never have existed."

Best of Appetizers

Mushrooms In Garlic Butter

From the Brunch Cookbook

This recipe is similar to those used for escargot. Be sure to make plenty because people who are timid about eating snails are bold when it comes to these mushrooms!

2 dozen large fresh mushrooms
    (about 1-1/2 inches in diameter)
1/2 cup butter
2 cloves garlic, minced
2 shallots, minced

1/2 cup minced parsley
1/2 tsp. fresh lemon juice
1/2 tsp. salt
1/4 tsp. pepper

Wipe or rinse mushrooms clean and remove stems. Discard stems or save them for another use. Combine butter, garlic, shallots and parsley in the workbowl of a food processor or in small mixing bowl. Process or mix until combined. Add lemon juice, salt and pepper. Blend briefly. Place mushrooms in a shallow baking dish. Fill each mushroom cap with a dollop of the garlic butter mixture (about 1/2 or 1 tsp.). Bake at 400°F. for 10 to 12 minutes, or until bubbly. Serve with crusty French bread, if desired. Use toothpicks to spear the mushrooms. Urge guests to dip bread into the remaining butter. Provide small plates and plenty of napkins. Makes 6 to 8 appetizer servings.

Avocado-Stuffed Eggs

From The Brunch Cookbook

For an extra special effect, spoon the filling into a pastry bag and pipe it decoratively into the eggs.

12 hard-cooked eggs
1 ripe avocado, peeled and seeded
1/2 tsp. garlic salt
1/2 tsp. dry mustard
1/2 tsp. each salt and pepper
1 tsp. mayonnaise

Cut each egg in half lengthwise. Remove yolks and combine with avocado, beating until light and fluffy. Add garlic salt, dry mustard, salt, pepper and mayonnaise. Beat until smooth. Fill eggs with mixture, using a pastry bag or a spoon. Dust the tops with cayenne (if you like spicy eggs) or paprika. Garnish with parsley. Refrigerate until serving time. Makes 24.

Sausage Appetizers

1 package precooked tiny smoked sausages
1 can crushed pineapple
1 cup brown sugar
2 T. prepared mustard
2 T. lemon juice

Drain pineapple, save the syrup. Combine pineapple, 2 T. syrup, brown sugar, mustard and lemon juice. Marinate sausages in this mixture for 2 hours. Skewer and broil over hot coals until crispy on the outside. Baste with marinade while cooking.

Chicken Teriyaki Strips

From Cocktails and Hors d'Oeuvres

This is an unusual and delectable marinade for chicken. The addition of mandarin oranges lends color to the hors d'oeuvre table. Pamper your guests and accompany this with a Polynesian-type drink. The consensus will be . . . encore!

1 can (11 ozs.) mandarin oranges
1-1/2 lbs. boneless chicken breasts
1/2 cup soy sauce
1 garlic clove, minced
2 tsp. maple syrup

1/4 cup water
1/4 cup wine vinegar
1/4 cup Madeira wine
3 T. applesauce
1/4 tsp. ginger

Drain oranges. Cut chicken into chunks or cubes. Combine remaining ingredients and pour over chicken. Marinate for 1/2 to 1 hour. Skewer chicken cubes, alternating with orange segments. Broil for a few minutes on each side, turning skewers to cook evenly. Brush several times with marinade. For best results broil just before serving so chicken does not become dry. Keep warm on a hot tray. Serves 4 to 6 guests.

Shanghai Meatballs

From Wok Appetizers and Light Snacks

The tenderness of meat can be improved by mixing in a proper choice of vegetables. So those who claim, "Our hamburgers are pure beef, no fillers!" are misleading you because the cost of adding vegetables may be more than using cheap ground beef. Certainly the final product is much lighter, more delicious and nutritionally balanced too.

1 lamb chop
2 lbs. ground beef
1/4 cup grated onions
2 tsp. salt
1/4 cup fresh breadcrumbs
2 T. milk to soak the crumbs
1 T. soy sauce mixed in milk
1 strip bacon, partially cooked, finely chopped
1/4 cup grated carrots
1 egg, unbeaten
1 cup breadcrumbs, for coating
1 egg, lightly beaten for coating crumbs
oil for deep-frying

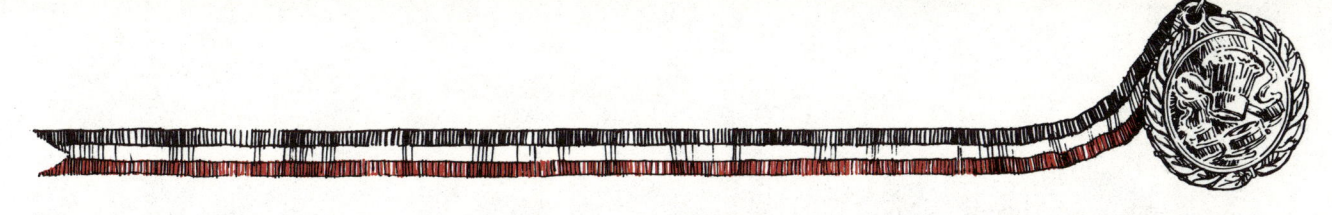

Broil lamb chop. Remove meat from bone and finely chop or grind it. Combine lamb with all remaining ingredients except breadcrumbs, 1 beaten egg and oil. Form into 1-inch balls. Coat the balls with crumbs, beaten egg and crumbs again. Heat oil in wok to 325°F. Fry for one minute. Meatballs can also be baked in a pan (leave space between the balls) in the oven at 350°F. for about 15 minutes. Actual time required in oven varies. Test them for doneness. Meatballs won't be as round as when deep fried. 96 Meatballs.

Sesame Shrimp

From Wok Appetizers and Light Snacks

In conventional Chinese cooking, the finishing touch of a dish is to sprinkle some cooking wine and sesame oil on it. Both will add a pleasant flavor to almost any dish. Sesame oil will not be very useful in making appetizers, but sesame seed will create many interesting ones—fancy and flavorful. You might have to visit a Chinese store to get black and white sesame seed, mixed in a ratio of 5 parts white to 1 part black.

about 3/4 lb. cooked shrimp
1 egg white
2 strips bacon, finely chopped
1 T. cornstarch

about 10 slices fresh bread
1 cup sesame seed
oil for frying

Finely chop shrimp. Mix with egg white, bacon and cornstarch. Chill for 30 minutes. Trim crusts from bread. Cut bread to whatever shape you like, preferably an odd shape, different from the rest of the appetizers so it will be distinctive—be creative! Pile a small amount of shrimp mixture on bread. Press seeds onto the mixture firmly so they will stick when fried. Heat oil in wok to 325°F. Fry appetizers until the white seeds are lightly brown. Serves 10

Skewered Shrimp, Avocado and Scallops

From Cocktails and Hors d'Oeuvres

A luxurious trio dipped in a sauce that has been tinged with vodka – it's mouthwatering.

1/2 lb. scallops
lemon juice
butter
1 large ripe avocado

1/2 lb. cooked shrimp
1 cup mayonnaise
1 T. vodka

Place scallops in a baking pan. Dab with lemon juice and butter. Broil for 5 minutes on each side. Cool. Cut avocado in half and remove skin and seed. Cut avocado into chunky pieces. Sprinkle liberally with lemon juice. Lace shrimp, avocado and scallops alternately on skewers. Mix mayonnaise and vodka together. Spoon into a small bowl. Serve on a circular plate with the sauce for dipping in the center. Makes 10 to 12 servings.

Seviche

From Favorite Seafood Recipes

This raw fish appetizer is very popular in Japan and certain South American countries. The lime juice, in which it marinates actually firms the fish and turns it opaque. Serve as a first course on lettuce leaves in cocktail cups or in a wide bowl at cocktail time for help yourself service.

1 lb. fresh white fish (red snapper, blackfish, flounder or turbot)
1 cup fresh lime juice
1 ripe tomato, diced
1/4 cup sliced green onion
1 can (4 ozs.) diced green chiles or sliced stuffed green olives
1/4 tsp. ground oregano
salt and pepper to taste
cilantro or parsley, chopped (optional)

Cut fish into small cubes. Arrange in a single layer in a glass dish. Add remaining ingredients, except cilantro. Stir well. Cover and chill for at least 6 hours, or until fish turns completely white. Serve garnished with cilantro. Makes 10 to 12 servings.

Mini-Reuben Sandwiches

From Cocktails and Hors d'Oeuvres

The Reuben is easy to make and always enjoys a good reputation. Try making half with just the corned beef and Gruyere cheese, and the other half the more traditional way, with sauerkraut. Each will earn raves.

1 cup well-drained sauerkraut
2 T. chopped, mild onion
softened butter
1 loaf party rye bread

1/2 lb. corned beef, sliced very thin
Russian dressing
1/2 lb. Gruyere cheese

Combine drained kraut and onion until well mixed. Butter both sides of bread slices. For half of hors d'oeuvres, place ingredients on bottom slice of bread in this order: corned beef, Russian dressing, kraut mixture and cheese. Use only corned beef and cheese on the other half. Top with remaining slices of bread and grill slowly until cheese melts and bread browns. Cut in half and serve. These can be made ahead and grilled just before serving. Keep warm on a hot tray. Serves 6 to 8 guests.

Cheddar Cheese Fondue with Apples

From The Fondue Cookbook

3 T. butter
3 T. flour
1 cup milk
2 cups (8 oz.) diced sharp, cheddar cheese
crisp, green apples

Melt butter in fondue pot over medium heat. Stir in flour. Let bubble a minute. Remove from heat. Slowly stir in milk. Return to heat and cook, stirring, until mixture thickens and boils. Add diced cheese. Stir until melted and smooth. Eat by spearing bite-size chunks of crisp, green apples on forks and dipping into mixture. Makes 6 servings.

Pecan Spread

From Easy Microwave Cooking
Men really go for this unbelievably easy dip.

1 pkg. (8 ozs.) cream cheese
2 T. milk
1/4 cup finely chopped green pepper
1/2 tsp. garlic salt
1/4 tsp. pepper

2 T. dry onion flakes
1/2 cup sour cream
1 T. butter
1/2 cup coarsely chopped pecans
1/2 tsp. salt

Put cream cheese in a large soup bowl or small casserole suitable for serving. Microwave 45 seconds on low (10%) power or just until softened. Add milk, green pepper, garlic salt, pepper, onion flakes and sour cream. Mix well. Place butter in a cup. Microwave 30 seconds on medium (50%) power to melt. Add nuts and salt. Stir well. Spoon over cheese mixture. Serve at room temperature or microwave about 1 minute on high (100%) power to serve warm. Serve with a variety of crackers or firm chips. Makes 2 cups.

Best of Soups

Spring Bounty Soup

From Creative Soups & Salads

Herald springtime with this picturesque green and gold soup.

2 T. butter
1 leek, white part only, chopped
2 cloves garlic, minced
1 carrot, sliced on the diagonal
2 T. flour
4 cups chicken stock
1/2 lb. asparagus tips and stems
   peeled and diagonally sliced

1 package (10 ozs.) tiny peas or fresh
   shelled green peas
1 dozen pea pods, strings removed and
   cut in half, diagonally
2 T. minced parsley
salt and pepper to taste
1/2 tsp. dried tarragon
grated Romano cheese

Melt butter in a large sauce pot. Saute leek, garlic and carrot until tender-crisp. Add flour and saute 2 minutes. Add stock and bring to boil. Add asparagus, peas and pea pods. Simmer 4 to 5 minutes, until asparagus is tender-crisp. Add parsley, season with salt, pepper and tarragon. Ladle into bowls. Sprinkle cheese on top. 6 servings.

Creamy Red Pepper Soup

From Creative Soups & Salads

This sprightly pale-red soup makes an appealing first course. Garnish with a fresh sprig of basil.

3 large sweet red peppers
1 T. olive oil
1 onion, chopped
3 cups chicken stock
1 clove garlic, minced

1/2 tsp. paprika
salt and freshly ground black pepper
3 T. tomato paste
1/3 cup whipping cream
basil leaves or chives, chopped, for garnish

Place peppers on their sides on a sheet of foil. Bake in a 450ºF. oven for 20 minutes, turning as the skin blackens. Remove from oven. Place in a paper bag and let set 20 minutes. Peel off skin. Cut peppers in half and remove seeds. Chop coarsely. In a large saucepan heat oil and saute onion until limp. Add chicken stock, peppers, garlic, paprika, salt, pepper and tomato paste. Bring to a boil. Cover and simmer 20 minutes. Let cool slightly. Puree in a food processor or blender. Blend in cream. Heat through or refrigerate. Serve in bowls garnished with basil or chives. 4 servings.

Soupe Au Pistou

From Creative Soups & Salads

1 qt. chicken stock
1 large boiling potato, peeled and diced
1 carrot, peeled and sliced
1/3 lb. fresh green beans, cut in 1-inch lengths
1 medium zucchini, thinly sliced
1 yellow crookneck squash, thinly sliced
1 leek, white part only, cut lengthwise and sliced
1/3 cup freshly shelled peas or tiny frozen peas, thawed
2 tomatoes, peeled and chopped
1 T. chopped parsley
Basil Parmesan Sauce: see below

Using a large saucepan, heat stock. Add potatoes, carrot and beans. Simmer 8 minutes. Add zucchini, crookneck and leek. Simmer 5 minutes longer. Add peas, tomatoes and parsley. Simmer 2 minutes longer. Ladle into soup bowls. Top with a spoonful of Basil Parmesan Sauce. 4 servings.

Basil Parmesan Sauce: Stir together 3 tablespoons chopped fresh basil, 1/4 cup Parmesan cheese, 1 tablespoon olive oil and 1 clove garlic, minced.

Sengalese Apple-Curry Soup

From Fast and Delicious

3 T. butter
1-1/2 cups tart apple, peeled, cored, and
  coarsely chopped
3/4 cup coarsely chopped onion
3 stalks celery, coarsely chopped
2 to 3 tsp. curry powder
salt and pepper, to taste
3 T. all-purpose flour
1 qt. chicken broth

3 whole cloves
1 large cinnamon stick
1 cup plain yogurt or sour cream
2 T. minced green onion, for garnish
  (optional)
2 T. shredded cooked chicken, for garnish
  (optional)
1/2 cup tart apple, in matchstick pieces,
  for garnish (optional)

Melt butter in saucepan over medium heat. Saute apples, onion and celery in butter until soft, about 8 minutes. Add curry, salt, pepper and flour. Saute 2 minutes more. Slowly add chicken broth, cloves and cinnamon stick. Reduce heat, cover and simmer 15 minutes. Cool slightly. Remove cinnamon stick and cloves. Puree mixture in food processor or blender if a smooth consistency is desired. Just before serving, place soup over medium heat. Add yogurt and stir until well blended. Garnish with minced onion, shredded chicken and matchstick apples if desired. Serves 6.

Orange Carrot Soup

From Creative Soups & Salads

Try this delicious soup either hot or cold.

5 carrots, peeled and sliced
1 large onion, peeled and coarsely diced
2 cloves garlic, minced
2 cups chicken stock
1/2 cup orange juice

1/8 tsp. freshly grated nutmeg
salt and freshly ground pepper to taste
1 tsp. grated orange or lemon peel
3 T. whipping cream or sour cream
1/4 cup coarsely chopped pistachios

Place carrots, onion, garlic and stock in a large saucepan. Bring to a boil. Cover and simmer 15 to 20 minutes or until vegetables are tender. Let cool slightly. Puree in food processor or blender. Blend in orange juice, nutmeg, salt, pepper, grated orange peel and cream. Reheat or refrigerate and serve chilled. Ladle into bowls and garnish with pistachios. 4 servings.

Babci's Chicken Soup

From Healthy Cooking on the Run

1 chicken, 3 to 4 lbs.
water
1 onion, sliced
1 cinnamon stick
4 each whole cloves and whole allspice
1 tsp. chopped parsley

1/2 head cabbage, cut in small wedges
1 carrot, sliced thin
1/2 tsp. dill weed
1/2 tsp. salt (optional)
2 raw potatoes cut in small pieces

Place chicken in large pot. Add water to cover, onion, cinnamon, cloves and allspice. Bring to boil, reduce heat and simmer uncovered 1-1/2 to 2 hours. Strain broth and remove chicken from bones. Cut into small pieces and refrigerate. Skim fat (this is easier if you chill the stock overnight). Add remaining ingredients to degreased broth and cook 45 minutes. Add chicken and cook 15 minutes. Serve in heated bowls. 6 servings.

Creme Calcutta

From Food Processor Cookbook

Terrific! Serve with chicken salad and hot rolls or French bread.

3 cans (10-3/4 ozs.) double-strength
   chicken broth
1 qt. water
1/2 cup uncooked rice
4 large onions

1/2 cube butter
3 tsp. curry powder
1 cup light or heavy cream
chopped parsley, tarragon,
   chopped cashews or toasted coconut

Heat chicken broth and water in a 4-quart pot. When boiling, stir in rice. Cook 20 minutes. Peel onions, and cut into chunks. Using steel blade, chop onions in two or three batches. Melt butter in large skillet. Add onion, and cook over medium heat until transparent. Stir occasionally. Do not allow to brown. Add curry powder. Cook 10 minutes longer. When onions are soft and a rich yellow color, add to rice mixture. Cook together 20 minutes longer. Using steel blade process warm soup, 2 cups at a time, until pureed. Just before serving, add cream. Serve garnished with parsley, tarragon, and a sprinkling of cashews or coconut. Makes 8 generous servings.

San Francisco Cioppino

From Creative Soups & Salads

1 stalk celery, diced
1 carrot, diced
1 leek, white part only, minced
2 green onions, chopped
2 T. olive oil
2 cloves garlic, minced
1/2 tsp. each dried basil and oregano
1 can (20 ozs.) tomato puree
1 cup clam juice or fish stock
1/2 cup dry white wine or vermouth

1/2 tsp. salt
1/4 tsp. freshly ground pepper
1 dozen small hard-shelled clams
1 lb. red snapper fillets or other
    white fish fillets, cut in 1-inch pieces
1/2 tsp. grated lemon or orange peel
2 T. minced parsley
1 large Dungeness crab, cooked
    and cracked

In a large saucepan, saute celery, carrot, leek and onions in oil until limp. Add garlic, basil, oregano, tomato puree, clam juice, wine, salt, and pepper. Bring to a boil and simmer 15 minutes. Add clams, fish, lemon or orange peel. Simmer 8 to 10 minutes more or just until fish flakes when prodded with a fork. Add crab and heat through. Sprinkle with parsley. Ladle into bowls. Serve with hot steamy hand towels for wiping fingers. 6 servings.

Black Bean Soup

From Creative Soups & Salads

Top this soup with sour cream and accompany with a trio of condiments. The lime wedges complement its peppery liveliness.

2 stalks celery, chopped
1 onion, chopped
2 T. olive oil
2 cups black beans
2 qts. water
3 cloves garlic, minced
1 small red dried pepper, seeds removed

1 tsp. ground coriander
1/4 tsp. ground cloves
1 tsp. salt
1 lb. cooked Polish sausage, sliced
Garnishes: sour cream, cilantro sprigs, lime wedges and shredded Monterey Jack cheese

In a skillet, saute celery and onion in oil until limp. Place beans, water, garlic, pepper, coriander and cloves in a large saucepan. Bring to a boil. Cover and simmer 1-1/2 to 2 hours or until beans are tender. Add salt. Add sausage and heat through. Ladle into bowls. Top with sour cream. Pass small bowls of cilantro, lime wedges and cheese to garnish the soup. 6 servings.

Cold Zucchini Soup

From No Salt, No Sugar, No Fat Cookbook

The hottest summer day can be improved by a cup of chilled soup. And, as anyone who has ever grown zucchini will tell you, you can never have enough recipes for zucchini.

1 cup sliced zucchini
1 clove garlic, chopped
1/2 cup nonfat milk
1 cup plain low fat or nonfat yogurt

Place all ingredients in blender container. Blend 30 seconds. Serve chilled. Makes 2 servings.

Seafood Gumbo A La Bundy

From Favorite Seafood Recipes

There are many versions of Gumbo. The traditional, southern method uses a roux (a "paste") made from oil and flour. This produces a somewhat heavy flavor, which many non-southerners are not used to. For a lighter taste, use butter instead of oil. The Commander's Palace, a fine restaurant in New Orleans, uses no roux at all. The chef there prefers a simple seafood broth. You should be able to find gumbo file at almost any gourmet foods store.

2 lbs. fresh crabmeat
1 lb. raw shrimp
1 pint shucked oysters
3/4 cup oil or butter
2/3 cup flour
1 cup chopped onion
4 cloves of garlic, minced
1 can (16 ozs.) tomatoes, chopped
1 bay leaf

1 tsp. chopped parsley
1-1/2 tsp. salt
1 sprig thyme (or 1/8 tsp. ground)
1 hot pepper pod, or dash cayenne
1-1/2 lbs. fresh okra, sliced or, 2 pkg.
   frozen sliced okra
1/4 tsp. gumbo file powder
boiled rice to serve 10

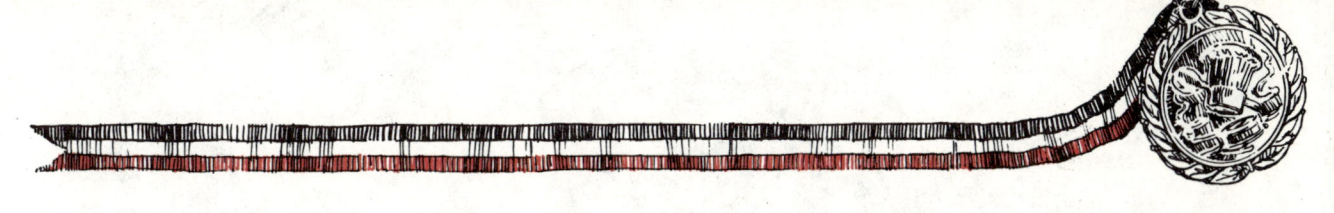

Pick out and discard any cartilage in crabmeat. Shell and devein shrimp. Drain oysters and reserve their liquor. In a large soup kettle, bring 3 quarts of water to a boil. In a separate pan, heat oil or melt butter. Add flour. Heat until mixture bubbles. If you are using oil, mixture must turn a dark brown. Do not let it burn, however. Add onions and garlic. Cook over low heat 4 minutes. Add roux to boiling water. Add tomatoes, bay leaf, parsley, salt, thyme, pepper, okra and oyster liquor. Simmer over very low heat at least 2 hours. Gumbo may be prepared up to this point a day in advance. 20 minutes before serving, add seafood. 5 minutes before serving, add gumbo file. Serve in warm soup bowls over rice. Makes 10 servings.

Best of Entrees

Best of Entrees

Chicken Baked in Tomato-Almond Puree

From New Ways to Enjoy Chicken

1 chicken, 3 lbs.,
   cut into serving pieces
1 cup lime juice
1-1/2 tsp. salt
1 can (17 ozs.) tomatoes, drained
2 whole cloves
6 peppercorns

2 bay leaves
1/4 cup water
1/3 cup vegetable oil
2 slices French bread,
   each 1-1/2 inches thick, cubed
1 cup blanched almonds
tomato and avocado slices (optional)

Marinate chicken pieces in lime juice and 1 teaspoon salt for one hour. Combine tomatoes, cloves, peppercorns, bay leaves, water and 1/2 teaspoon salt in blender or food processor. Puree. Pour oil in skillet. Place over medium-high heat. Fry bread cubes in oil until golden, about 2 minutes on each side. Drain on paper towels. Add cubes to tomato mixture. Saute almonds in oil until golden. Add almonds to tomato mixture. Puree mixture until smooth. Spread 1/3 of puree mixture in shallow baking dish. Remove chicken from marinade and arrange in dish over puree mixture. Cover with remaining puree. Bake uncovered, at 350°F. until chicken is tender, about 45 minutes. Garnish with tomato and avocado slices, if desired. Makes 4 servings.

Chicken with Italian Sausages and Pasta

From Quick & Easy Pasta Recipes

Tender nuggets of chicken and mild Italian sausages make a delicious hearty pasta main course.

8 ozs. dried pasta (small bow ties or fettuccine)
3 mild or hot Italian sausages
1/4 cup white wine or water
3 chicken breast halves, skinned and boned
flour, salt and pepper to coat chicken
2 T. butter
3 T. minced shallots
1 cup chicken broth
1/2 cup tomatoes, peeled, seeded and chopped
2 to 3 T. coarsely chopped pimiento
salt and pepper to taste
2 T. minced parsley

Place sausages and white wine in a small saucepan. Cover and bring to a boil. Simmer 5 minutes. Uncover and prick sausages to release fat. Increase heat to evaporate liquid and lightly brown sausages. When sausages cool, cut into 1/2-inch rounds. Cut chicken breasts into 1-inch squares. Dust lightly with seasoned flour. Melt butter in medium size skillet over medium heat. When foaming, add chicken and saute until lightly browned, about 2 mintues on each side. Remove from pan. Reduce heat to low and add shallots. Stir for a minute. Add chicken broth and stir to remove browned bits from bottom of pan. Bring to boil. Add chicken pieces, sausages, chopped tomato, pimiento, salt and pepper. Stir for 1 minute to heat through. Place hot, drained pasta in a large heated bowl. Add sauce and toss to combine. Sprinkle with parsley. Serve immediately on warm plates. 4 servings.

Chicken with Savory Noodle Stuffing

From Quick & Easy Pasta Recipes

Buttery egg noodles, spinach and sausage make a savory stuffing for roast chicken. Roasting chicken at this high temperature produces a crisp brown skin.

3 ozs. medium dried egg noodles
3 T. butter
3/4 cup finely diced celery
4 to 6 green onions, thinly sliced
1 clove garlic, minced

6 ozs. fresh spinach, coarsely chopped
3/4 cup diced cooked Italian or link sausage
salt
1/4 tsp. white pepper
1 roasting chicken, 4 to 4-1/4 lbs.

Cook noodles according to package directions. Drain well. Melt butter in skillet. Saute celery, onions and garlic until soft but not brown. Stir in spinach and saute until wilted. Add diced sausage, drained noodles, salt and pepper. Mix well. Stuff chicken and tie with kitchen string. Roast on a rack in a 450°F. oven for approximately 1 hour and 15 minutes. Pour a small amount of water in bottom of roasting pan to keep juices from burning. Let rest 10 minutes before carving. 4 to 6 servings.

Almond-Encrusted Chicken

From New Ways to Enjoy Chicken

Crunchy almonds add interest to this simple dish. After you roll the chicken in almonds, this dish may be refrigerated for up to 24 hours.

2 eggs
1 cup milk
1 tsp. salt
1 tsp. paprika
flour
1 chicken, 2-1/2 to 3 lbs., cut into serving pieces
1 cup sliced almonds
1/2 cup vegetable oil

Beat eggs lightly with milk, salt and paprika. Dip chicken pieces, one at a time, into flour, then into egg mixture. Roll in almonds. Pour oil into shallow baking dish. Arrange chicken pieces in pan, skin side up. Bake at 375°F. for 1 to 1-1/2 hours, basting twice during baking process. Makes 4 servings.

Rum Chicken

From Fast and Delicious

This recipe can be served hot or at room temperature.

one 3-pound chicken cut into small pieces, or use thighs, drumsticks and wings
1/4 cup fresh lime juice (fresh is important)
1/3 cup rum (white is preferable)

3 T. soy sauce
2 large cloves garlic, crushed
all-purpose flour
lime wedges, for garnish (optional)

Toss chicken with lime juice. In a plastic bag, combine rum, soy sauce and garlic. Add chicken and lime juice and let mixture marinate in refrigerator for several hours or overnight. Drain. Dredge chicken in flour, shaking off excess. You can omit the flour step if you are in a hurry. Place chicken in a shallow pan. Bake at 350°F. for 45 minutes, or until done. Serve with lime wedges if desired. Serves 4 to 6.

Timesaver: If you don't have time to marinate the chicken for several hours, marinating it for an hour (or less) at room temperature works almost as well. If you do that, the flavor of the recipe is improved by making the marinade into a sauce. To do this, add 1-1/2 tablespoons of cornstarch to 1/4 cup water. Mix until smooth. Add to marinade. Heat in a saucepan until mixture thickens and is bubbly. Serve as a sauce with the chicken.

Sour Cream Baked Chicken

From New Ways to Enjoy Chicken

A simple dish whose rich sour cream and mustard sauce qualifies it as a company meal. Prepare it with a gourmet mustard for a special treat.

1/2 cup sour cream
1/4 cup prepared mustard
1 tsp. salt
1/4 tsp. rosemary leaves, crushed
1/8 tsp. black pepper
2 chickens, 3 lbs. each, cut into serving pieces
2-1/2 cups fresh bread crumbs
1/2 cup melted butter

Combine sour cream, mustard, salt, rosemary and pepper. Mix well. Spread mixture over chicken pieces, coating well. Roll chicken in bread crumbs. Arrange in shallow baking dish. Drizzle with half of butter. Bake at 375°F. for 30 minutes. Remove from oven and drizzle with remaining butter. Bake 30 minutes more, or until chicken is golden brown and done. Makes 6 to 8 servings.

Indian Chicken

From No Salt, No Sugar, No Fat Cookbook

1 frying chicken, cut up or your
   favorite parts
2 cloves garlic, minced
2 tsp. freshly grated ginger
1-1/2 T. curry powder or to taste
1 tsp. paprika
1 tsp. garam marsala*
2 T. lemon juice

2 T. flour
2 T. finely chopped green onion
2 T. chopped fresh parsley
1 cup plain low fat or nonfat yogurt
chopped tomatoes
chopped water chestnuts
lemon or lime wedges

Remove skin from chicken. Combine remaining ingredients, except chopped tomatoes, water chestnuts and lemon wedges. Coat chicken with mixture. Cover and allow to marinate for several hours or overnight in the refrigerator. Arrange chicken pieces in single layer in a shallow pan. Bake uncovered in 350°F. oven for about 50 minutes or until chicken is tender. Serve over cooked rice or bulgur wheat. Garnish with tomatoes, water chestnuts, lemon or lime wedges. Makes 4 to 6 servings.

*Mixture of ground cardamon, black pepper, cumin, coriander, cinnamon and cloves. Available in markets which carry Indian foods and spices.

Chicken in A Bag

From Easy Microwave Cooking

Paper bags are great in microwave ovens. The microwaves pass right through the bag, which eliminates all mess from spattering.

3 T. catsup	3 T. brown sugar
2 T. Worcestershire sauce	1 tsp. salt
1 T. vinegar	1 tsp. dry mustard
1 T. lemon juice	1 tsp. paprika
2 T. butter	2-1/2 to 3 lb. chicken parts

Mix all ingredients except chicken in a large glass baking dish or Corningware pan. Microwave 2 minutes, stirring often. Dip chicken into sauce and place in a clean brown bag. Fold end over and slip in a second bag. Place on a large platter. Microwave 18 to 21 minutes (7 minutes per pound). Let rest a few minutes before serving. Makes 4 to 6 servings.

Mock Veal — Turkey

From Healthy Cooking on the Run
Quick, easy, tasty, nutritious and low-calorie! Serve with rice and a green vegetable.

1 lb. young turkey breast slices, pounded lightly
flour
1 tsp. oil
1 tsp. margarine
1/2 cup sliced mushrooms
1 green onion, sliced
1/2 tsp. thyme
1/2 fresh lemon
lemon slices

Dredge turkey slices in flour. Heat oil and margarine in skillet. Brown turkey. As turkey is browning add mushrooms, onion and thyme. Squeeze lemon juice over turkey slices and remove from skillet. Stir mixture remaining in skillet until blended and slightly thickened. Spoon over turkey slices. Garnish with lemon. 4-6 servings.

Pasta with Scallops and Red Peppers

From Quick & Easy Pasta Recipes
Red peppers are a pleasant contrast to the pasta and scallops in flavor as well as visually.

12 ozs. fresh pasta or 8 ozs. dried pasta
2 medium size fresh red bell peppers
2 T. butter
3 T. minced shallots
1 cup cream

1/4 tsp. white pepper
1 lb. scallops, cut in half if large size
salt to taste
2 T. butter for pasta
2 T. minced parsley

This is a very fast sauce, so time the pasta to be done approximately 6 minutes after you start the sauce. Cut red peppers along ridges and remove membrane and seeds. Using a swivel blade vegetable peeler, remove outer skin from pepper sections. Cut in thin slivers or julienne. Melt butter in medium skillet. Saute shallots 1 minute. Add cream and white pepper. Turn heat on high and reduce cream 2 to 3 minutes until it starts to thicken. Reduce heat to medium. Add scallops and salt. Cook 1 minute. Add red peppers and cook 1 minute. Toss hot, well-drained pasta with 2 tablespoons butter and about half of the scallop mixture. Top with remaining scallops and parsley. Serve on warm plates. 3 to 4 servings.

Crunchy Baked Fish

From No Salt, No Sugar, No Fat Cookbook
Crispy "fried" fish without fat or spatter.

1 whole (1-1/2 to 2 pounds) trout, sole or flounder
1/4 cup whole wheat flour
1/4 cup Grape Nuts cereal
1/2 tsp. garlic powder
1/2 tsp. onion powder
1 T. chopped fresh parsley
1/2 cup plain low fat or nonfat yogurt

Rinse fish under running water and remove scales. Mix dry ingredients and parsley together. Dip fish in yogurt, then in flour mixture. Place on foil-lined shallow baking dish that has been preheated. Bake at 400°F. for 20 to 25 minutes. For a crisper crust, brown under broiler for 2 to 3 minutes. Garnish with lemon. Makes 4 servings.

Broiled Fillets with Tangerine Sauce

From Favorite Seafood Recipes

1 lb. firm white fish fillets
1 T. butter or margarine, melted
1 T. tangerine or orange juice
salt and pepper

Place fillets in a single layer in a well-greased baking pan. Combine melted butter with juice. Brush over fish. Sprinkle with salt and pepper. Broil fish 10 minutes per inch of thickness. Baste once during broiling with pan juices. Arrange fish on a warm serving platter. Serve with Tangerine Sauce. Makes 2 to 4 servings.

Tangerine Sauce: Saute 1/4 cup sliced almonds in 2 tablespoons butter. Mix 1 tablespoon cornstarch with 1/2 cup tangerine or orange juice in a 1-quart saucepan. Add 2 tablespoons each white wine, apple jelly and lemon juice. Cook, stirring, until mixture thickens. Add a dash of hot pepper sauce, pinch of salt, 1/2 teaspoon grated tangerine or orange rind, 1 tangerine or orange, peeled and cut into small pieces, and the sauteed almonds and butter. Heat and serve with broiled fillets. Makes 1 cup.

Swordfish Stuffed with Lobster

From Fisherman's Wharf Cookbook

6 slices swordfish
1/2 pound butter
1/2 cup celery, minced
1 onion, chopped
3/4 pound lobster meat, minced
1 cup chicken stock
1/2 tsp. poultry seasoning
salt and pepper

1-1/2 cups fine bread crumbs
3 eggs
Caper Sauce:
4 T. capers
1/4 cup Sauterne
2 cups cream sauce
4 T. Parmesan cheese

Cut a pocket into the side of each steak. (Cut from the side but not clear through.) Set aside. Melt butter in a skillet and saute celery, onion, and lobster for 3 minutes. Add chicken stock, poultry seasoning, salt and pepper. Add bread crumbs and mix thoroughly. Remove from heat. Beat eggs slightly with a fork and add to mixture until it is smooth.

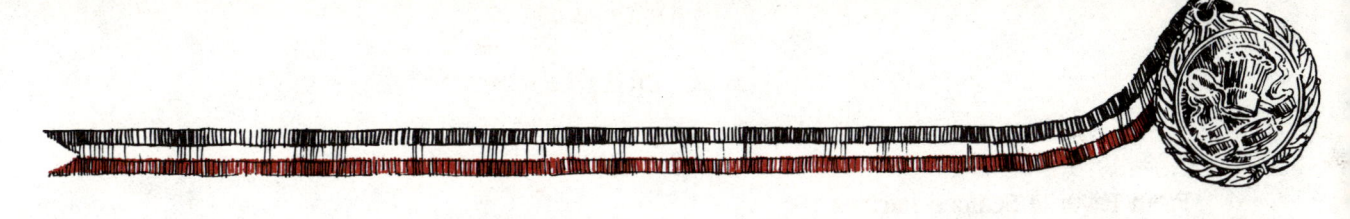

Spoon stuffing into swordfish pocket, reserving a small amount. Spread a thin layer of the stuffing on top of each steak. Place in a buttered pan and broil until brown, then lower the heat to 375°F. and bake in oven for 25 minutes. (Or until the fish flakes when pricked with a fork.)

Caper Sauce: Saute capers in wine and add to cream sauce. Whip well and set aside. When fish has baked, place it carefully into a casserole. Ladle the caper sauce over the fish, sprinkle with Parmesan cheese, and brown. 6 servings.

Sole Surprises

From Favorite Seafood Recipes

1-1/2 to 2 lbs. sole fillets (8 pieces)
1/4 lb. small shrimp, cooked, shelled
   and deveined
1/4 cup fine dry bread crumbs
1/2 tsp. fine herbes
1/4 tsp. onion salt

1/4 tsp. dill
1/4 cup grated Parmesan cheese
3 T. mayonnaise
1 can cream of shrimp soup, undiluted
2 T. dry sherry
chopped chives, for garnish (optional)

Dry fish with paper towels. Grease 4, six-ounce Pyrex custard cups. Arrange two pieces of fish in an ''X'' pattern in the cups. Make sure to have the fillets touching the sides and bottom of the cups. Fillets will overlap and hang out the sides of the cups quite a bit. Stir together shrimp, bread crumbs, fines herbes, onion salt, dill, Parmesan cheese and mayonnaise. Divide mixture among fillets and stuff. Fold excess fish over filling, completely enclosing the filling. Bake at 350°F. for 30 to 40 minutes. Just before fish is done, heat soup and sherry together in a saucepan. When fish is done, turn cups upside down on a serving platter. Spoon sauce over fillets. If desired, sprinkle with chives. Makes 4 servings.

Gourmet Flatfish

From Favorite Seafood Recipes

A classic duxelle mixture, which consists of mushrooms, onions and herbs, bakes beneath any fish from the flatfish family.

1 T. salad oil
1 T. flour
1/4 cup finely chopped mushrooms
1/3 cup finely chopped onions
3/4 tsp. crushed tarragon leaves
1/4 cup dry white wine, or fish stock
1/4 cup cream or milk

2 lbs. flatfish fillets (such as turbot, dab, fluke or sole), skins removed
salt, pepper and paprika to taste
1/4 cup dry bread crumbs
2 T. melted butter
1 cup shredded, mild cheese

Pour oil into a 13 x 9 x 2-inch baking dish. Stir in flour. Sprinkle mushrooms, onions and tarragon over flour. Stir in wine and cream. Dry fillets with paper towels. Place them over duxelles mixture. Combine salt, pepper, paprika and bread crumbs. Sprinkle over fish. Pour melted butter over crumbs. Bake at 425°F. for 10 minutes per inch of thickness. Add cheese the last 5 minutes of baking. Makes 4 to 5 servings.

Italian Broiled Shrimp

From Fast & Delicious

Back in ''the good ol' days'' . . . when shrimp was inexpensive, we enjoyed this dish frequently. It is fantastic eating. Try substituting fresh (not frozen) bay scallops for shrimp for a superb variation.

18 to 24 large (jumbo are better) shrimp, peeled
2 T. all-purpose flour
1/4 cup butter
1/4 cup olive oil

Drawn Butter Sauce:
4 T. butter
2 T. all-purpose flour
salt and freshly ground pepper
2 tsp. fresh lemon juice
1 cup hot water
2 T. finely chopped garlic
1/4 cup fresh chopped parsley
1/2 tsp. oregano

Dust shrimp generously with flour. In a flat broiling pan, melt 1/4 cup butter under broiler. Add oil and heat until bubbly. Place shrimp in pan, coat with butter-oil mixture. Broil under heat about 3 minutes. Shrimp will not be done. Prepare Drawn Butter Sauce. Melt 2 tablespoons butter in saucepan over medium heat. Add flour, salt and pepper. Stir well. Whisk in lemon

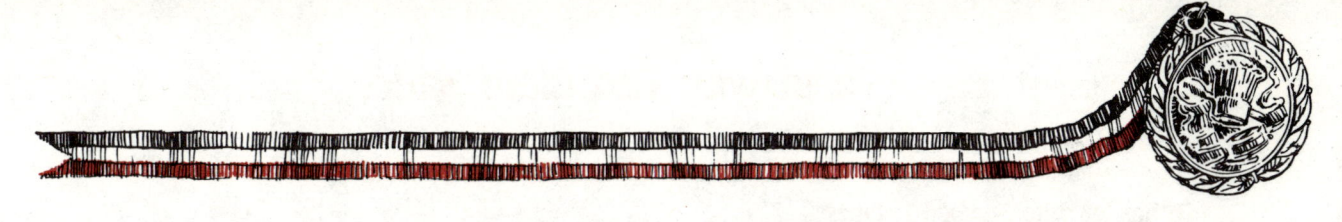

juice and water. Cook about 5 minutes. Add remaining 2 tablespoons butter and stir until melted. Just before removing from heat, add garlic, parsley and oregano to sauce. Heat about 1 minute. Pour over broiled shrimp and stir until shrimp are coated. Return shrimp to broiler and broil under high heat 3 to 4 minutes, or just until shrimp turn pink. Serve with plenty of French bread to soak up that marvelous sauce. Serves 6.

Pasta with Red Clam Sauce

From Favorite Seafood Recipes

Any firm-fleshed fish such as halibut or rock cod can be substituted for the clams.

12 ozs. fresh pasta or 8 ozs. dried pasta
1 T. olive oil
1 small onion, finely chopped
1 clove garlic, minced
1 can (28 ozs.) Italian-style tomatoes
1/2 tsp. anchovy paste (optional)
2 T. tomato paste
2 tsp. sugar
1/2 tsp. each dried sweet basil, thyme and oregano
2 cans (6-1/2 ozs. each) chopped or minced clams
salt and pepper to taste

Time pasta to be done when sauce is ready. Heat oil in medium size saucepan. Add onion and garlic and saute 4 to 5 minutes until onion is translucent. While onions are cooking, empty

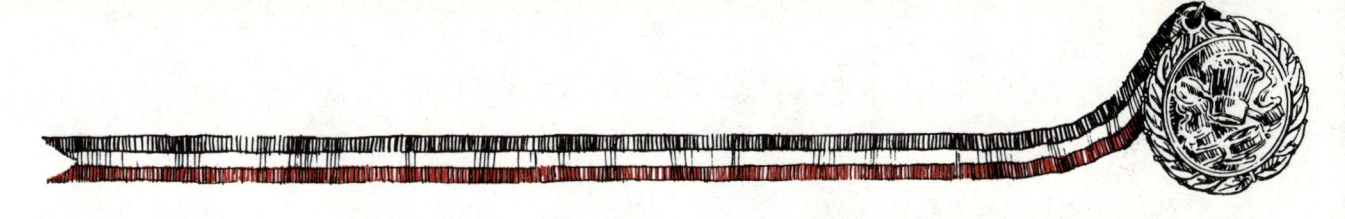

tomatoes into sieve over a bowl. Cut tomatoes in half. Squeeze out most of the seeds. Trim away hard core and chop tomatoes coarsely. Add tomatoes and 1/2 cup of the tomato juice to saucepan. (Reserve remaining tomato juice for another use.) Add anchovy paste, tomato paste, sugar, sweet basil, thyme and oregano to saucepan. Drain clams. Set clams aside and add clam juice to saucepan. Bring to boil. Cook uncovered over medium heat for approximately 20 minutes until sauce reduces and starts to thicken. Add clams and heat. Serve immediately over hot, well-drained pasta on warm plates. 3 to 4 servings.

Note: If fish is substituted for clams, lightly flour the fish and saute in 2 to 3 tablespoons olive oil. Cut into cubes and add to tomato sauce.

Pepper Steak with Cream

From The Barbecue Cookbook

2-1/2 to 3 lbs. fillet or top sirloin steak
2 tsp. salt
1/4 cup peppercorns, cracked
3 T. oil
1/4 cup brandy
1 cup cream
minced parsley

Remove the fat and bone from the steak, sprinkle with salt. Press the pepper into both sides of the steak. Brown on top of the stove in hot oil for 1 minute on each side. No longer. This is simply to secure the peppercorns and to get some meat juices for your sauce. Place on the grill over medium coals, turning occasionally until done. Test with knife after 10 minutes. Add brandy to the hot oil and drippings in your frying pan. Ignite. When flame has died, add cream and stir until thick. Place steak on a platter and pour the cream sauce over. Sprinkle with parsley. Serves 4.

Pot Roast Pacific

From Extra Special Crockery Pot Recipes
Teriyaki seasonings richly flavor and glaze this chuck roast.

4 to 5 lb. chuck roast
2 to 3 T. olive oil
4 cloves garlic, minced
1 cup pale dry sherry
1/3 cup soy sauce

1 T. chopped fresh ginger or
   1-1/2 tsp. ground ginger
freshly ground pepper
2 green onions, thinly sliced
4 whole cloves

Rub roast with about 1 tablespoon oil and the minced garlic. Place meat in a glass or stainless bowl. Add sherry, soy, ginger, pepper, onions and cloves. Turn meat to coat. Cover and chill overnight. To cook, remove meat from marinade. Save marinade. Pat meat dry with paper towels. Brown well on both sides in 1 to 2 tablespoons olive oil. Transfer to crockery pot. Add 1/2 cup reserved marinade. Cover. Cook on low (200°) 7 to 8 hours or until fork tender. Transfer to platter and keep warm. Add 1/2 cup more marinade to pan juices. Cook down until reduced. Pour into sauce bowl. Makes 8 to 10 servings.

Barbecued Hamburgers

From Healthy Cooking on The Run

Serve with potato salad, a tossed green salad and sliced tomatoes.

Sauce:
1 T. margarine
1/2 cup chopped onion
1/4 cup catsup
3 T. vinegar
1 T. sugar
1 T. Worcestershire sauce
1 tsp. paprika
1 tsp. mustard
1/4 tsp. Tabasco sauce (optional)

Hamburgers:
1 lb. lean ground beef
1 cup soft bread crumbs
1 egg, lightly beaten
1/4 cup minced onion
2 T. milk
1 T. prepared horseradish
1/2 tsp. salt
1/2 tsp. dry mustard

To make sauce, melt margarine in saucepan. Add onions and cook until tender. Stir in remaining ingredients and simmer 15 minutes. Gently mix hamburger ingredients and form into 6 patties. Brush patties with sauce. Broil 5 minutes on one side. Turn and broil 3 minutes on the second side. 4 to 6 servings.

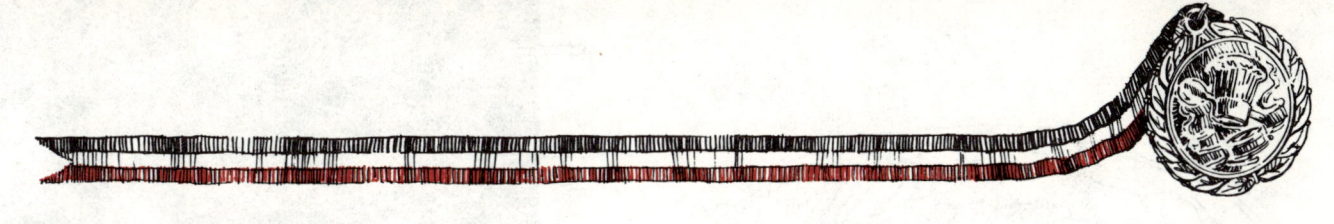

Variations for hamburgers:

Chop onions coarsely and increase to 1/2 cup
Add 1/2 cup chopped green peppers
Add 1 cup chopped spinach
Replace bread crumbs with 3/4 cup cooked rice (Porcupine patties)
Replace 1/2 of the ground meat with cottage cheese
Add 1 tablespoon minced parsley and 1/4 cup grated Parmesan cheese

Meat Sauce with Zucchini

From No Salt, No Sugar, No Fat Cookbook

Absolutely delicious served over pasta or grains. This also makes an excellent topping for a pizza.

1/2 cup chicken or vegetable stock
3/4 cup chopped onion
1 clove garlic, minced
2 cups cubed zucchini
1/2 pound very lean ground beef

2 cups tomato sauce
1 T. fresh basil or 1/2 tsp. dried basil
1/2 cup chopped fresh mint
1/4 tsp. dried chili pepper (optional)
freshly ground pepper

Heat stock in saucepan. Add onions and garlic and saute until tender. Add zucchini. Cover and simmer until zucchini is just tender, about 5 minutes. Brown meat in hot skillet and drain all fat. Add meat, tomato sauce and seasonings to zucchini mixture. Simmer over low heat for 10 minutes. Makes 4 servings.

Barbecued Roast in Foil

From The Barbecue Cookbook

2 onions, sliced
3 T. chopped celery
3 carrots, sliced
1 clove garlic, crushed
2 T. butter
1/4 cup soy sauce
1/2 cup tomato sauce
1 T. prepared mustard
1 tsp. salt
1 tsp. pepper
4-5 lb. rolled roast

Saute onion, celery and carrots with garlic in butter for 7 minutes. Combine soy sauce, tomato sauce, mustard, salt and pepper and add to vegetables. Brown beef on all sides over the coals. Put part of vegetable sauce on a large piece of heavy-duty foil. Place meat in center of foil and cover with rest of sauce. Fold foil over meat, sealing edges so no juice can escape. Cook over low coals, turning occasionally for 1-1/2 to 2-1/2 hours. Serves 8.

Chili

From Healthy Cooking on The Run

1 lb. lean ground turkey, beef or
    veal
1 onion, chopped
1 cup fresh tomatoes or 1 can
    (7-1/2 ozs.) tomatoes
1 can (8 ozs.) tomato purée
1 cup water

2 cups cooked or canned kidney beans,
    drained
2 tsp. chili powder
1/4 tsp. salt (optional)
1/2 tsp. each garlic powder, oregano
    and ground cumin
1/4 tsp. pepper

Break up meat and cook in large non-stick skillet until no pink remains. Drain off fat. Add remaining ingredients. Bring to boiling and reduce heat. Cover and simmer 45 minutes or slow cook in a crock pot, or in a 225°F. oven 6 to 8 hours. Slow cooking develops flavor in chili, but this chili turns out surprisingly well when quickly made in a microwave oven. Leftovers are even better after being reheated.

Microwave: Break meat into a round microwave-safe dish. Microwave on High 5 minutes. Drain off fat. Add remaining ingredients except beans. Microwave covered, 10 minutes. Add beans and stir. Microwave 3 minutes. 6 to 8 servings.

Mexican Crepes

From Crepes & Omelets

Corn Chip Crepes filled with chili flavored meat and cheddar cheese, topped with a sauce of fresh tomatoes and avocados.

8 Corn Chip Crepes, page 76
3/4 lb. ground beef
1/4 cup catsup
1/4 tsp. dry mustard
1/4 tsp. chili powder

1 T. taco sauce
salt and pepper
1/2 cup water
1 cup grated cheddar cheese
Tomato Avocado Sauce, page 75

Make crepes as directed and set aside. Saute meat in skillet. When browned and finely crumbled, drain off excess fat. Add catsup, mustard, chili powder, taco sauce, salt and pepper. Pour in 1/2 cup water. Simmer on low heat, uncovered, until mixture is quite dry.

Fill Corn Chip Crepes with meat mixture. Sprinkle cheddar cheese on meat mixture. Roll crepes, place in lightly greased, ovenproof serving dish. Heat in 350°F. oven for 10 to 15 minutes. Serve with Tomato Avocado Sauce. Makes 4 servings.

Tomato Avocado Sauce

From Crepes & Omelets

2 ripe avocados
2 ripe tomatoes
2 to 3 green onions
4 to 5 T. chopped fresh cilantro
1/2 tsp. salt
pepper to taste

Peel, seed and dice avocados and tomatoes. Thinly slice green onions. Combine avocados, tomatoes, green onions, cilantro, salt and pepper. Let stand at room temperature 20 to 30 minutes before serving so mixture becomes juicy. Stir occasionally. Makes sauce for 8 crepes.
Note: Mexican Crepes freeze well. Fill crepes, place in foil pan, cover and freeze. To defrost, place foil covered pan in 375°F. oven 30 to 35 minutes.

Corn Chip Crepes

From Crepes & Omelets
These are similar to corn tortillas and delicious with Mexican-type fillings.

2 eggs
2 T. vegetable oil
1 cup milk
1/3 cup water
1/2 cup all-purpose flour
1 cup loosely-packed, crushed Fritos corn chips
1/4 tsp. salt

Place all ingredients in blender or food processor container in the order listed. Cover and blend at high speed 20 to 30 seconds. Scrape down sides of the container. Blend a few more seconds. Cook, following directions on page 77. Stir batter occasionally to prevent Fritos from settling to the bottom. Makes 14 to 16 6-inch crepes.

Directions for Cooking Crepes

From Crepes & Omelets

Crepe pan is at the correct temperature when the batter sizzles slightly when poured into the pan, and a crepe will cook on one side in approximately 1 minute. Crepes should be pale in color, not dark brown.

2 or 3 T. of batter is usually enough to cover the bottom of a 6 to 7 inch crepe pan. Pour in the batter and quickly tilt the pan so the batter covers the bottom entirely. The crepe is ready to turn when it begins to set and is crisp around the edges. Loosen around the edge with a spatula or knife and carefully turn.

Stack cooked crepes on a plate. They will be easier to separate if they are not placed squarely on top of each other. It is not necessary to put foil or waxed paper between each crepe. Crepes will keep several days in the refrigerator or can be frozen stacked and wrapped in foil or plastic. They will pull apart easily when they are defrosted and warmed slightly.

Pork Chops in Orange Sauce

From Extra-Special Crockery Pot Recipes
Pork chops gain a shiny rich glaze and tartness with this sauce.

4 thick center-cut pork chops
salt and pepper to taste
1 T. butter
1/3 cup each orange juice and catsup

1 T. orange marmalade
1/2 tsp. grated orange peel
1 orange, sliced
watercress for garnish (optional)

Season chops with salt and pepper. Brown well in butter in a large frying pan. Transfer to crockery pot. Pour orange juice and catsup into pan drippings. Stir in marmalade and orange peel. Boil 1 minute. Pour over chops. Cover. Cook on low (200°) 6 to 8 hours. Remove chops to warm platter. Slash orange slices to center. Twist and arrange one slice on each chop. Tuck a bouquet of watercress alongside. Pass sauce. Makes 4 servings.

Glazed Sausage Striped Meat Loaf

From Extra-Special Crockery Pot Recipes
Potatoes cut ''French fry'' style bake around this juicy meat loaf.

3 (about 3/4 lb.) mild Italian sausages
2 eggs
1/2 cup milk
2 slices bread
1 tsp. each salt and Worcestershire
1 tsp. dry mustard
1 tsp. beef stock base
1 small onion
1-1/2 lbs. ground beef chuck
1/4 cup catsup
1 tsp. Dijon-style mustard
1-1/2 T. brown sugar
4 large boiling potatoes
2 T. soft butter

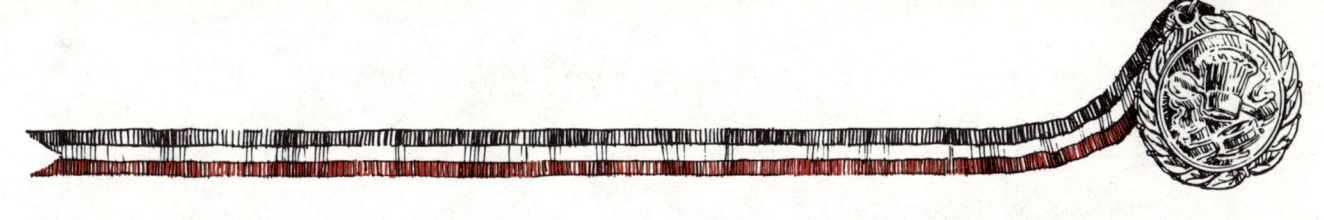

Simmer sausages in water to cover 10 minutes. Drain. Place eggs, milk, bread, salt, Worcestershire, dry mustard, stock base and onion in blender container. Cover. Blend until smooth. Place ground meat in mixing bowl. Pour in blender contents. Mix until smooth. Pat half of meat loaf mixture in the bottom of crockery pot. Cover with sausages. Top with remaining meat loaf. Pat to seal. Combine catsup, mustard, and brown sugar. Spread over meat. Peel potatoes. Cut in strips. Coat well with butter and place around meat. Cover. Cook on high (300°) 1 hour. Reduce to low (200°) 6 hours. Serves 8.

Vegetable Stew

From No Salt, No Sugar, No Fat Cookbook

This vegetable dish is especially nice to make in the fall when the last of the garden vegetables are too good to throw out, but not pretty enough to serve raw. It freezes nicely and will be a delight to serve on a dreary winter day.

1 cup dried white beans
3 cups water
3 to 4 green onions, chopped
1 to 2 cloves garlic, minced
1/2 cup chopped celery
4 medium tomatoes, coarsely
    chopped

1 small green pepper, chopped
1 to 2 teaspoons fresh basil or 1/2 tsp.
    dried basil
2 zucchini, chopped
freshly ground pepper
parsley (for garnish)

Rinse beans and soak overnight in 3 cups of water. The next day, cook beans in soaking water for 1 hour. Mix remaining ingredients, except zucchini, with the beans. Transfer to casserole. Cover and place in preheated 350°F. oven. Bake for 1-1/2 hours. Add zucchini. Continue cooking uncovered for 20 to 30 minutes. Add pepper. Garnish with parsley, if desired and serve. Makes 8 to 10 servings.

Mandarin Ham Rolls

From Fast & Delicious
Even people who don't like ham enjoy this dish.

2 cans (11 ozs. each) mandarin oranges, drained
2 cups cooked rice
1/3 cup mayonnaise
3 T. each chopped pecans, parsley and green onions
12 large slices boiled ham
1/2 cup orange marmalade
2 T. fresh lemon juice
1/2 tsp. ginger

Reserve 12 orange sections. Toss together remaining oranges, rice, mayonnaise, pecans, parsley and green onions. Place a large spoonful of mixture in center of each slice of ham. Roll slices. Place seam side down in a baking dish just large enough to hold rolls. Combine marmalade, lemon juice and ginger. Brush rolls with this mixture. Bake at 350°F. for 25 minutes. Garnish with reserved oranges. Serves 6.

Pasta Primavera

From Quick & Easy Pasta Recipes

12 ozs. fresh or 8 ozs. dried tagliarini, spaghetti or fettuccine
4 T. olive oil
1 small onion, finely chopped
1/4 tsp. red pepper flakes
1/2 lb. mushrooms, thinly sliced
1 clove garlic, minced
1 cup diagonally sliced asparagus or green beans
1 cup cauliflowerets
1 medium-size yellow squash, thinly sliced
1 medium-size red or green pepper, peeled and cut in thin strips
1 cup coarsely grated carrots
2 medium-size tomatoes, peeled, seeded and coarsely chopped
1/2 cup fresh blanched or frozen peas
salt and pepper to taste
3 T. parsley, finely chopped
1/3 cup Parmesan cheese

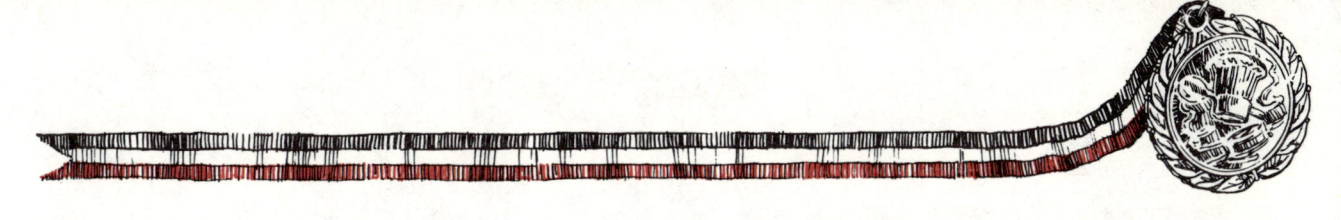

Start heating pasta cooking water in large pot. Time pasta so it is cooked when the sauce is finished. Heat olive oil in a large skillet. Saute onion and red pepper flakes for 3 to 4 minutes. Add mushrooms and garlic. Cook for 2 minutes over medium-high heat. Add asparagus pieces, cauliflowerets, yellow squash and peppers. Cover and cook 2 minutes. Add carrots, tomato pieces, peas, salt and pepper. Cook 2 to 3 minutes. Toss with hot, well-drained pasta. Top with parsley and Parmesan cheese. Serve immediately on warm plates. 3 to 4 servings.

Country Sausage

From Food Processor Cookbook

Making sausage is easy with a food processor. What a pleasure to season it just the way you like. And you'll have juicy sausage to serve without a panful of fat to throw out! This is my favorite recipe.

2-1/2 lbs. lean country ribs or pork loin end roast
2 tsp. salt
1 tsp. ground pepper
1 tsp. grated fresh ginger root
    or 1/2 tsp. ground ginger
1 tsp. crumbled dried sage leaves
    or 1/2 tsp. powdered sage or poultry seasoning
1/2 tsp. sugar
1/4 tsp. ground cloves

Cut pork, including fat, into 1/2 by 1-inch pieces. There should be about 4 cups. Combine salt, pepper, ginger, sage, sugar and cloves. Sprinkle over pork pieces and stir to blend. (Mixture can be refrigerated for one to two days, if desired.) When ready to make sausage, insert steel

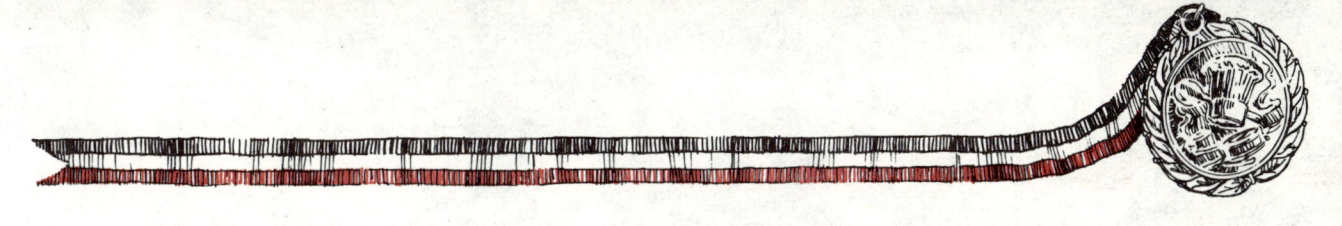

blade in processor bowl. Add about 1 cup pork pieces and process 30 to 40 seconds. (Meat hitting the blades makes a smooth sound when it is uniformly chopped. If you should notice a loud sound, stop processor. Check blades for small pieces of bone or cartilage.) Transfer ground pork to a mixing bowl. Repeat until all pork is chopped. Shape into 8 large patties or 16 to 20 small ones. Brown over medium-high heat. Reduce heat to medium or low as patties cook on second side. Small patties take 10 to 15 minutes to cook, and the large ones about 20 minutes. Makes 8 servings.

Note: Set pork bones aside for some other use, such as barbecued bones, to cook with sauerkraut, or for beans with pork, etc.

Best of Brunch Dishes & Light Entrees

Crispy French Toast

From The Brunch Cookbook

Cornflakes make a crispy crust; serve with a tangy sour cream sauce. Bacon or sausage makes a nice side dish.

1 cup evaporated milk
3 T. water
1 egg
1 tsp. vanilla
1 T. sugar
1/2 tsp. salt
1/2 tsp. cinnamon

10 slices day-old bread
2 cups cornflake crumbs
Strawberry Sour Cream Sauce:
1 pkg. (10 ozs.) frozen strawberries, thawed
1 cup sour cream
1/2 tsp. nutmeg
1/2 tsp. cinnamon

Combine evaporated milk, water, egg, vanilla, sugar, salt and cinnamon in a shallow dish. Beat well. Dip bread into this mixture and then into cornflake crumbs. Brown toast on both sides on a lightly buttered griddle over medium-high heat. While French Toast is browning prepare Strawberry Sour Cream Sauce. Stir all ingredients together in a small bowl. Spoon over hot toast. Serves 6.

Grandma's Oatmeal Hotcakes

From The Brunch Cookbook

2 cups rolled oats
2 cups buttermilk
3 eggs, beaten
2 T. sugar
4 T. melted shortening

1/2 scant cup all-purpose flour
1 tsp. baking powder
1 tsp. baking soda
1 tsp. salt

Stir oats and buttermilk together in a bowl. Cover and let stand on counter overnight. The next morning, add eggs, sugar and melted shortening. Stir well to combine. Sift flour, baking powder, soda and salt into oatmeal mixture. Stir until just combined. Cook on a lightly greased hot griddle until bubbles appear and underside is golden brown. Turn once. 12 hotcakes.

Country Style Omelet

From Crepes & Omelets
A hearty omelet made with potatoes and served flat.

6 slices bacon
1 large baking potato
5 to 6 green onions, thinly sliced
2 tomatoes
1 T. butter
2 T. chopped parsley
6 eggs
2 tsp. water
4 drops Tabasco
salt and pepper

Cut bacon into small pieces. Fry until crisp in a 9-inch ovenproof skillet. Remove bacon and set aside. Peel and cut potato into 1/4-inch dice. Saute slowly in bacon fat. When almost done add green onions and cook until potatoes are lightly browned and onion is wilted. Drain excess

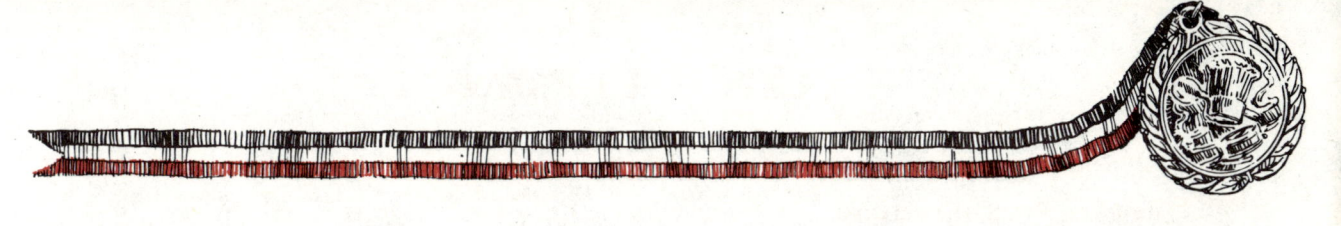

fat from skillet. Peel, seed and chop tomatoes. Melt butter in a small saucepan. Cook tomatoes over fairly high heat for 3 to 4 minutes until most of juice has evaporated. Spread potatoes and onion evenly around skillet. Sprinkle with bacon. Add cooked tomatoes and chopped parsley. Beat 6 eggs with water, Tabasco, salt and pepper. Pour eggs over potato mixture. Cook over low heat until eggs start to set. Lift around sides of the pan so the uncooked portion flows under the cooked part. Place under broiler as far away from heat as possible for 5 to 10 minutes until top is set and lightly browned. Slide out of pan onto serving plate. Cut in wedges to serve. Makes 4 servings.

Variations: Omit bacon. Fry potatoes in vegetable oil and use sliced salami, diced ham, thinly sliced Italian sausage, smoked salmon, or sardines.

Omit tomato and use 3/4 cup grated Swiss cheese, or Parmesan cheese.

In addition to onion, add green pepper, green chilies, pimiento and fresh sweet basil or cilantro.

Quiche A La Provençale

From The Brunch Cookbook

If you have vegetarian friends, this quiche makes a delightful main dish. Add a simple green salad, fruit and cheese to complete your menu.

1 egg, lightly beaten
1 T. water
One 10-inch unbaked pie shell
1 pkg. (6 ozs.) long-grain and wild rice mix
2 T. olive oil
2 cloves garlic, minced

1 can (14 ozs.) Italian plum tomatoes
   (2 cups)
1 pkg. (8 ozs.) cream cheese
1 tsp. salt
1/4 tsp. pepper
4 eggs, lightly beaten

Beat 1 egg with 1 tablespoon of water to make a glaze. Brush about 1 tablespoon over pie shell and bake at 375°F. for 10 minutes. Remove from oven and set aside while making filling. Cook rice mix according to package directions. Heat olive oil in a small skillet over medium-low heat. Sauté garlic until limp. Combine hot cooked rice, garlic mixture, tomatoes, cream cheese, salt and pepper. Stir until cream cheese is melted. Stir a small amount of this hot mixture into 4 beaten eggs. Return egg mixture to the rice mixture and blend well. Pour into prepared crust

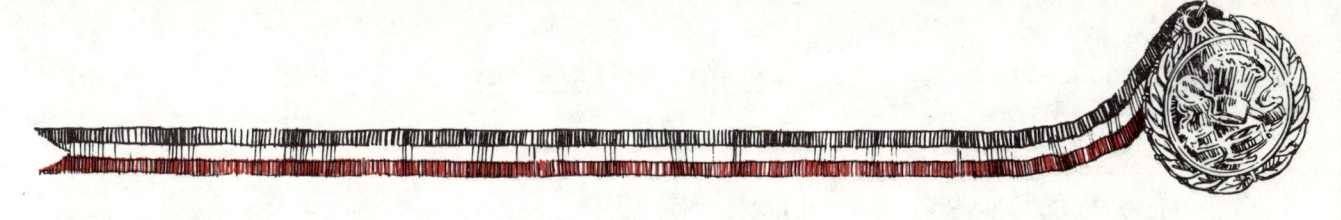

and bake at 375°F. for 30 minutes, or until set. Let stand for 10 to 15 minutes before cutting and serving. Serves 6.

Hint: At the Cordon Bleu in London they mince garlic by flattening it with the side of a knife along with a generous teaspoon of salt. Continue to press and chop the garlic and salt mixture together until garlic is very finely crushed. This method works well in this recipe. If you use this method, however, don't forget to reduce the amount of salt in the recipe by 1 teaspoon.

Salmon Mousse

From No Salt, No Sugar, No Fat Cookbook

1 envelope plain gelatin
2 T. lemon juice
1 small onion, sliced
1/2 cup boiling water
1/4 tsp. paprika
1 tsp. dill weed
2 cups cooked salmon or 1 can (16 ounces) salmon
1 cup plain low fat or nonfat yogurt

Pour gelatin into blender container. Add lemon juice, onion and boiling water. Blend 40 seconds. Add paprika, dill and salmon. Blend briefly. Add yogurt and blend 30 seconds longer. Pour into mold and chill. Unmold by placing in hot water for 45 seconds. Turn out on lettuce-lined platter and garnish as desired. Fresh dill is especially nice, if available. Makes 4 to 5 main dish servings.

Seafood Frittata

From The Brunch Cookbook

Frittatas are open-faced Italian omelets. They are cooked slowly over very low heat until firm and set, but not dry or stiff. Make them round and cook them on both sides. Cheese, vegetables, herbs, seafood and various meats are among the fillings used for Frittatas.

6 eggs
1/4 tsp. each salt and pepper
3 T. butter
1/4 cup coarsely chopped onion
1/2 cup sliced mushrooms
1/4 lb. tiny bay scallops
1/4 lb. fresh cooked crab
1/4 lb. fresh cooked shrimp
1 cup grated Parmesan or Swiss cheese
3 T. butter

Beat eggs in a bowl. Add salt and pepper. Set aside. Melt butter in a heavy-bottomed skillet

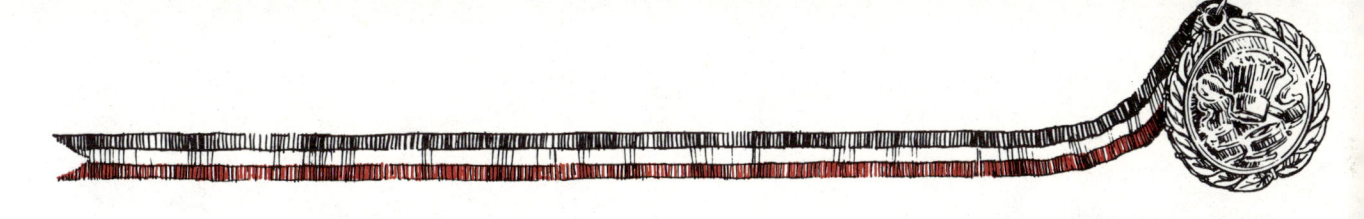

over medium heat. Sauté onion and mushrooms in butter until limp. Add scallops and cook for just a few minutes, until opaque. Stir crab and shrimp into skillet. Remove pan from heat. Stir about three quarters of the cheese into the eggs. Add cooked seafood mixture to egg and cheese mixture and blend thoroughly. Wipe skillet out with a paper towel. Add remaining 3 tablespoons of butter to skillet. Place over medium heat. When butter begins to foam, add egg and seafood mixture. Turn heat down to low. Cook eggs without stirring, until set and thickened, about 10 minutes. Preheat broiler.

When only the top is still moist, sprinkle with remaining cheese and place skillet under broiler until top is lightly golden brown. Loosen Frittata with a spatula and slide it onto a warm plate. Cut into wedges and serve. Serves 4 to 6.

Sour Cream Pancakes

From Muffins, Nut Breads & More

1 cup whole wheat flour
1/2 cup wheat germ
2 T. unprocessed bran
1-1/2 tsp. baking powder
1/4 tsp. baking soda
1/2 tsp. salt
1/2 cup sour cream
1 egg, separated
2 T. honey or molasses
1-1/4 cups milk
3 T. melted butter, margarine or oil

Stir together flour, wheat germ, bran, baking powder, baking soda and salt. Mix sour cream, egg yolk, honey, milk and butter together well. Add this mixture to the dry ingredients. Stir until just moistened. Beat egg white until stiff. Fold into batter. Pour or spoon batter onto a hot griddle or frying pan. Cook on both sides until golden brown. Makes 10 to 12 medium-sized pancakes.

Backpackers Cereal

From No Salt, No Sugar, No Fat Cookbook

Take this along when traveling. It's much more nutritious than the prepackaged variety, and keeps well without refrigeration.

1/2 cup rolled oats
1/2 cup wheat flakes
1/2 cup barley flakes
1/2 cup instant nonfat dry milk
cinnamon, nutmeg to taste
dried fruit (raisins, chopped dates, bananas, apricots)

Spread grains in shallow pan and toast in 450°F. oven until brown, about 5 to 7 minutes. Watch closely to prevent overbrowning. Remove from oven, add dry milk and seasoning. Store in air-tight container. To serve, add hot water and mix. Top with fruit.

Sausage and Mushroom Strudel

From The Brunch Cookbook

Buttery, flaky pastry wraps around a creamy sausage and mushroom filling for an unusual and tasty treat. Purchase phyllo at your local delicatessen or in the gourmet section of your grocery store.

1 lb. bulk sausage
6 T. butter
2 T. oil
1 lb. fresh mushrooms, finely chopped
1/2 cup minced green onions
1 tsp. salt
1 tsp. pepper
1 pkg. (8 ozs.) cream cheese
12 sheets phyllo pastry
1 cup melted butter
1 cup fine dry bread crumbs.

Sauté sausage in a heavy skillet over medium heat until no pink remains. Drain thoroughly

and set aside. In another skillet, melt butter with oil over medium heat. Add mushrooms and green onions and cook, stirring until liquid has evaporated. Stir in salt and pepper. Add cooked sausage and cream cheese, blending thoroughly. Lightly dampen a tea towel. Lay a sheet of phyllo on the towel. Brush with melted butter and sprinkle lightly with bread crumbs. Repeat four times, ending with sixth sheet of phyllo. Place half of the filling on the narrow edge of the phyllo, leaving a two-inch border on each side. Fold in sides and roll up pastry. Place roll on a buttered baking sheet. Brush with additional melted butter. Repeat procedure using remaining phyllo and sausage filling. Bake at 400°F. for 20 minutes or until golden. Serves 6 to 8.

Fantastic Mushroom Eggs with Cheese and Cream Sauce

From The Brunch Cookbook

For the mushrooms:
2 T. butter
1 lb. fresh mushrooms, thinly sliced
salt, pepper—a dash each

For the eggs:
1 dozen eggs
1/2 cup butter
salt, pepper—a dash each

Melt 2 tablespoons of butter in a large skillet over medium heat. Sauté mushrooms until soft. Sprinkle with salt and pepper. Set aside. Break eggs into a large bowl and whisk thoroughly. Add salt and pepper. Melt half of the 1/2 cup butter in a large skillet over very low heat. Pour eggs into skillet. Gently scramble eggs. When eggs have turned into very soft curds, stir in remaining butter and sprinkle with salt and pepper. Set aside. Make a cream sauce and shred the cheeses:

Sauce:
6 T. butter
6 T. all-purpose flour
1 pint half-and-half
salt, pepper—a dash each

Cheeses:
4 ozs. Parmesan cheese, grated
4 ozs. Swiss or Gruyére cheese, grated
4 ozs. Cheddar cheese, grated or
    12 oz. of a combination of cheeses

Melt butter in a saucepan over medium-low heat. Stir in flour. Allow mixture to bubble for 30 seconds. Add salt and pepper. Stir in half and half. Whisk over low heat until mixture thickens.

To Assemble:

Lightly butter the bottom of a large ovenproof casserole. Sprinkle with half of the Parmesan. Spread a thin layer of the cream sauce over cheese. Place half of the scrambled eggs on top. Add half of the remaining cream sauce to mushrooms, stir. Place mushroom mixture on top of the eggs. Sprinkle with half of the grated Swiss and Cheddar. Add rest of eggs. Top with remaining cream sauce. Sprinkle with remaining Swiss, Cheddar and Parmesan. Broil 6 inches from the heat until cheese is bubbly and eggs are heated through. Serves 6 to 8.

Best of Vegetables

The Nitty Gritty Method for Cooking Green Vegetables

From The Fresh Vegetable Cookbook

This 7 minute method for cooking fresh peas, green beans, asparagus, broccoli and Brussels sprouts produces attractive, delicious vegetables which retain their bright green color. The secret is to have the water boiling when the vegetables are added and to keep it boiling during the entire cooking process as follows:

1. Bring a teakettle full of water to a full boil.

2. Into another pot with a lid, scatter a handful of sugar and 1 teaspoon of salt. Place over high heat until sugar begins to caramelize.

3. Quickly add prepared vegetables. Without reducing heat, pour in the boiling water. The water never ceases boiling and the vegetables start cooking immediately. Cover the pot and boil rapidly for exactly 7 minutes.

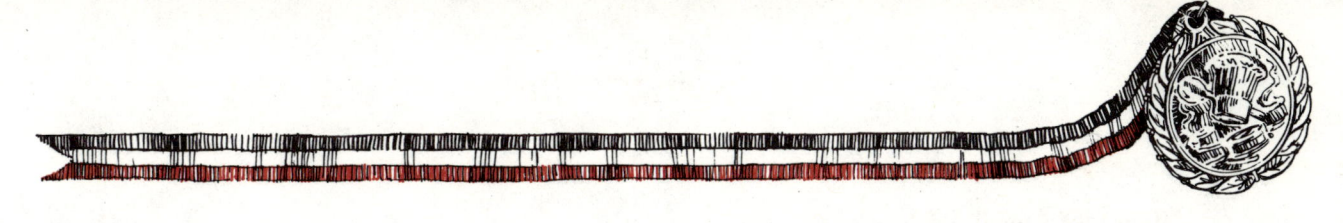

4. Quickly drain vegetables into a colander and rinse briefly with cool tap water to stop the cooking action. The vegetables will remain hot!

5. Drain well and season with melted butter or a sauce of your choice.

This method is not used for root vegetables, eggplant, artichokes or spinach.

Spinach Tart

From Easy Microwave Cooking

A delightful appetizer that also makes a delicious side dish.

2 T. butter
1/4 tsp. basil
1/4 tsp. oregano
1 small onion, finely chopped
2 cups shredded fresh spinach
1 T. all-purpose flour

1 cup shredded cheese, Monterey Jack,
    Muenster, or Cheddar
1 can (5 ozs.) evaporated milk
4 eggs, beaten
pinch nutmeg
pinch cayenne pepper
1 tsp. salt

Place butter in a glass cake or pie pan. Cook on medium-high (70%) power until melted, about 30 seconds. Add basil, oregano and onion. Cook 1 minute on high (100%) power. Add spinach. Cook 1 minute on high power. Mix together flour and cheese. Add remaining ingredients. Stir into onion mixture. Cook on medium power (50%) for 12 minutes, stirring after six minutes. Remove from oven. Allow to stand 10 minutes before serving. Makes 10 to 12 servings.

Orange Sweet Potato Souffle

From Quiche & Souffle Cookbook

6 cup, well-buttered souffle dish
1 lb. yams or sweet potatoes
1/4 cup butter
1/2 cup milk

3/4 cup Grand Marnier*
salt, pepper, pinch nutmeg
4 egg yolks
6 egg whites

Preheat oven to 375°F. Peel sweet potatoes. Cut in chunks. Boil in salted water 15 minutes. Drain well. Return to heat, shaking briskly to drive out any excess moisture. (Potatoes will appear floury). Force through food mill or other pureeing device. Beat in butter, milk and Grand Marnier. Season highly with salt, pepper, and nutmeg. Beat in egg yolks. Transfer to large bowl. Beat whites until stiff, but not dry. Fold gently into base. Pour into prepared dish. Bake in preheated oven until souffle has risen, appears well-puffed and is browned across the top. It will wobble slightly when shaken gently. Serve immediately. 6 to 8 servings.

*or other orange flavored liqueur.

Broccoli A La San Francisco

From The Fresh Vegetable Cookbook

2 lbs. broccoli
melted butter
Parmesan cheese
3 T. butter
3 T. flour
salt, cayenne pepper, celery salt
1 cup milk
1 T. lemon juice
3 T. orange juice
1 T. grated orange rind
1 tsp. grated lemon rind
heavy cream
blanched slivered almonds

Wash and trim broccoli. Remove tough portions of stems with a vegetable peeler. Cook according to the Nitty Gritty Method on page 108. Drain and quickly rinse in cold water to

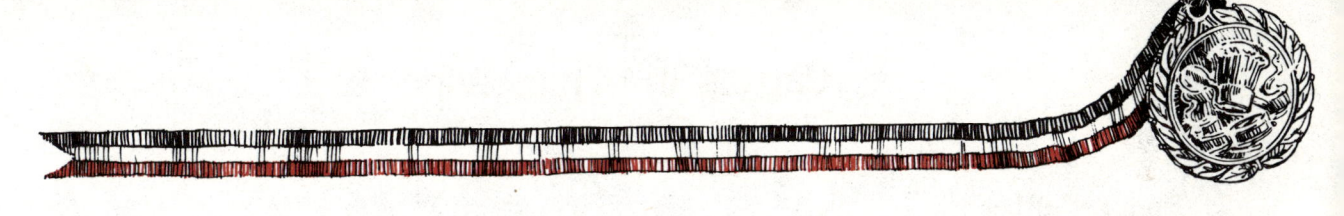

prevent further cooking. Drain thoroughly. Dip cooked broccoli in melted butter. Sprinkle liberally with Parmesan. Arrange on a flameproof serving dish. Melt 3 tablespoons butter in saucepan. Stir in flour, salt, cayenne and celery salt. Cook 1 minute. Remove from heat. Blend in milk. Return to heat and stir until mixture thickens and boils. Add juices, grated rinds and just enough cream to thin the sauce a bit and give it a creamy consistency. Spread carefully over broccoli. Bake in hot oven 425°F. until sauce and almonds are both browned and dish is bubbling. Serve immediately. Makes 6 servings.

Carrots in White Wine

From Fast & Delicious

2 pounds carrots, scraped and cut into 1/4-inch thick slices
1-1/2 cups diced celery; include some of the leaves
1/2 cup chopped onion
3/4 cup dry white wine
1/4 cup sugar
1/4 cup butter
1 tsp. dill
salt and pepper

In a large saucepan mix everything together. Cook, covered, over low heat, until carrots are just tender. Do not overcook. Serves 6 to 8.

Zucchini Puffs

From The Fresh Vegetable Cookbook

3 slices provolone cheese*
2 cups shredded zucchini
3 T. chopped onion
1/2 cup bread crumbs
1/2 tsp. salt

1/4 tsp. pepper
2 T. chopped parsley
2 eggs
oil

Grate cheese in blender or food processor, or chop finely. Remove stem ends from zucchini and shred finely. Press out as much moisture from zucchini as possible with paper towels. Combine with onion, crumbs, salt, pepper, parsley and eggs. Put 1 teaspoon of oil in each of twelve muffin cups. Heat in 375°F. oven 3 or 4 minutes. Carefully spoon batter into sizzling oil. Bake 20 minutes. Makes 12 puffs.

*Other cheese may be used, if desired.

Eggplant Torta

From The Fresh Vegetable Cookbook

1 large eggplant
seasoned flour
peanut oil
salt, pepper, thyme to taste
1/2 cup chopped parsley
6 large tomatoes
1 onion, finely chopped
2 green peppers, finely chopped
2 pkg (8 oz. ea.) sliced Mozzarella cheese
1 cup (1/2 pt.) whipping cream
1/2 cup half and half
3 eggs
2 egg yolks
nutmeg

Peel and slice eggplant. Dredge in seasoned flour. Fry in hot, deep oil until nicely browned

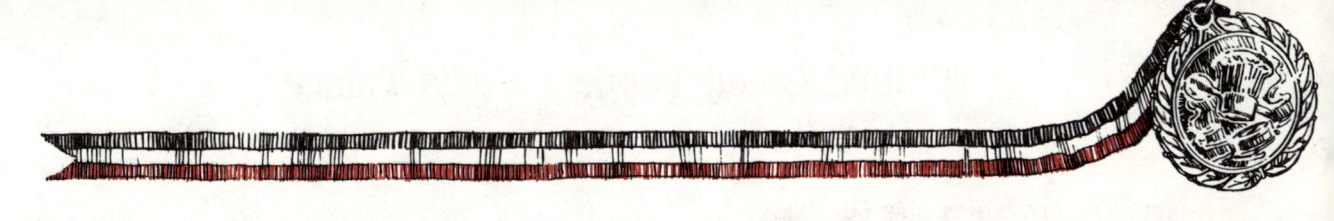

and soft. Place half the eggplant slices in a large oblong baking dish. Season with salt, pepper, thyme and 2 tablespoons chopped parsley. Peel, seed and slice tomatoes. Cover eggplant slices with half the tomatoes. Sprinkle tomatoes with salt, pepper, more parsley, half the onion and half the peppers. Cover with half the cheese slices. Repeat layers ending with cheese. Beat remaining ingredients together. Pour over layered ingredients. Bake in 425°F. oven 30 to 40 minutes or until the custard is completely set and cheese is deeply browned. Remove from oven. Let rest 5 minutes before serving. Makes 6 servings.

Stuffed Green Peppers Gallia Palace

From The Fresh Vegetable Cookbook

6 large green peppers
1 loaf (1 lb.) firm white bread
milk
2 cups cooked chicken breast, ground
1/2 cup pine nuts
1/2 cup light raisins
1 large egg, well beaten
salt and white pepper

Wash peppers. Slice off tops and remove seeds. Rinse insides and drain. Remove crusts from bread slices. Reduce to crumbs using blender or fingers. Add enough milk to crumbs to thoroughly moisten. Add remaining ingredients. Mix well and pack into peppers. Replace tops. Stand peppers in shallow baking dish with about 1 inch of stock or water. Bake in 350°F. oven about 30 minutes or until peppers are thoroughly cooked. Cool and serve at room temperature. Makes 6 servings.

Almond Noodles

From Fast & Delicious

10 ozs. medium-wide egg noodles (homemade if possible)
1/4 cup butter (not margarine)
1/3 cup slivered blanched almonds
1 T. poppy seeds
1 tsp. paprika
1 T. fresh chopped parsley
salt and pepper

Slightly undercook noodles in boiling salted water. They should still resist slightly when bitten. In a small skillet, melt butter over medium heat. Add almonds. Cook until golden. Add butter, almonds and remaining ingredients to drained noodles. Add a little more butter if mixture seems dry. Serve immediately. Serves 6.

Almond Crusted Potato Patties

From Food Processor Cookbook

Serve with poached or baked fish, or leg of lamb. Prepare ahead and reheat in the oven just before serving.

Dutchess Potatoes, page 121
2 T. soft or melted butter
1-1/2 cups sliced almonds

Prepare Dutchess Potatoes as directed. Butter a rimmed baking sheet. Spread almonds on waxed paper. Drop 6 rounded tablespoonfuls Dutchess Potato mixture, one or two at a time, onto almonds. Lift with fork or spatula to coat both sides of patties with almonds. Lay almond-coated patties on buttered pan. Patties can be refrigerated up to two days at this stage. Just before serving, bake in upper third of a 400°F. oven, 10 to 12 minutes or until almonds on bottom are brown. Turn patties. Bake 5 minutes longer. Will hold in oven, with heat off, if necessary. Makes 6 servings. If desired, make 12 small patties allowing 2 per serving.

Dutchess Potatoes

From Food Processor Cookbook

A favorite when entertaining because they taste good, look pretty and can be prepared ahead. Also attractive as a decorative border on creamy seafood or chicken casseroles, or piped around planked steak or fish.

3 medium potatoes
2 T. butter
2 egg yolks
1/2 tsp. salt

freshly ground white pepper
freshly grated nutmeg
2 T. melted butter

Cut potatoes in halves. Cook in water to cover, without salt, for 20 minutes. Drain well. With steel blade inserted in food processor bowl, purée potatoes. Add butter, egg yolks, salt, pepper and nutmeg. Process only until smooth. Place potato mixture in a 16-inch pastry bag, fitted, with large star tip (#4 Ateco). Pipe in decorative rings or ovals onto well-greased baking sheet. Refrigerate at this point, if desired. Just before serving, brush with melted butter. Heat in upper third of 400°F. oven 10 to 12 minutes, until browned on ridges.

Bulgur Wheat-Cheese Bake

From Fast & Delicious

1-1/2 cups raw bulgur wheat
2 T. butter
1 T. vegetable oil
1-1/2 cups chopped onion
2 cups sliced fresh mushrooms
2 cups minced green peppers
2 T. soy sauce

2 T. sherry
1/2 tsp. marjoram
salt and pepper
1-1/2 cups cottage cheese
3/4 cup crumbled Feta cheese
4 eggs, slightly beaten
paprika

Soak the bulgur wheat in 1-1/2 cups boiling water for 20 minutes. Drain. (This step cannot be omitted or bulgur wheat will not absorb the liquid in the casserole.) Melt butter in skillet over medium heat. Add oil. Saute onion, mushrooms and peppers until just tender. Remove from heat. Add soy sauce, sherry, marjoram, salt and pepper to vegetables. Spread bulgur evenly on the bottom. Cover with vegetables. Place mixed cheeses on top of vegetables. Pour beaten eggs with a little salt and pepper over everything. Sprinkle with paprika. Bake uncovered 45 minutes at 350°F. Let stand a few minutes before serving. Serves 6.

Fresh Cranberry Relish

From Food Processor Cookbook

Nice to share at holiday time. Makes a delightful "from-my-kitchen" gift.

2 small to medium red-skinned apples
1 large or 2 small oranges
3 cups firm fresh cranberries
1-1/2 cups sugar
1/8 tsp. salt
1/2 cup pecans, optional

Wash fruit. Quarter apples, and cut into chunks. Cut oranges, with rinds intact, into chunks. Remove seeds. With steel blade inserted in processor bowl, chop cranberries in two batches. Transfer to a large mixing bowl. Process apples and oranges, a few chunks at a time, until finely chopped, but not pureed. Empty each batch into bowl with cranberries. Add sugar and salt. Stir to blend. Place in covered container and refrigerate. Keep relish pressed below juices. A lovely red color develops as relish stands a few days. Will keep up to one month. At serving time sprinkle with chopped pecans, if desired. Makes about 6 cups.

Best of Salads

Bistro Salad

From Creative Soups & Salads

This superb green salad has just the right interplay of flavors and textures. Consider pairing it with Camembert, Brie or chevre for a combination salad-cheese course.

1 large head butter lettuce
1 bunch watercress, large stems removed
1 avocado
1 red Delicious or Winesap apple
1/4 cup chopped toasted filberts, sunflower seeds, walnut halves or
    toasted, slivered almonds
1 T. chopped parsley
1 T. chives or shallots
6 T. Vinaigrette Dressing, page 127

Tear lettuce into bite-size pieces. Combine with watercress sprigs in a large salad bowl. Peel and slice avocado. Peel, core, and slice apple. Arrange avocado and apple slices on top of greens. Scatter nuts and herbs over the top. Add dressing and mix lightly. Makes 4 to 6 servings.

Vinaigrette Dressing

From Creative Soups & Salads

Here is a basic, versatile dressing to make in quantity. Refrigerate it in a slender wine or vinegar bottle, a good design for shaking and pouring. Use it on green salads, shellfish, sliced tomatoes, raw mushrooms, cooked chilled asparagus, green beans, broccoli, cauliflower, zucchini, beets or other vegetables suited for a vinaigrette treatment. White wine vinegar is recommended for light-colored foods such as mushrooms.

1/2 cup olive oil
1/2 cup salad oil
6 T. red or white wine vinegar
1 tsp. salt
freshly ground pepper
1 T. Dijon-style mustard
3 shallots, peeled and chopped or 3 green onions (white part only)

Combine all ingredients in blender container. Cover and blend until smooth. Pour into a bottle and refrigerate. Shake well before using. Makes 1-1/2 cups dressing.

Deli Pasta Salad

From Quick & Easy Pasta Recipes

8 ozs. dried egg noodles
3 ozs. Mortadella, ham or bologna, thinly sliced
3 ozs. Gruyere or Swiss cheese, thinly sliced
1 large sour or German-style pickle
1 large or 2 small tart apples, peeled
1-1/2 T. Worcestershire sauce
3 to 4 T. mayonnaise
1/2 tsp. white pepper
2 T. freshly grated Parmesan cheese
2 T. parsley, minced

Cook noodles. Immediately drain and rinse with cold water. Drain well. Cut meats, cheese and pickle into strips approximately the same width and thickness as the noodles. Coarsely grate the apple. Combine noodles with meats, cheese, apple and pickle. Add Worcestershire sauce, mayonnaise, white pepper and grated cheese. Gently toss with two forks until well mixed. Refrigerate for at least two hours or overnight before serving. Garnish with minced parsley. 4 servings.

Chicken Salad In Orange Shells

From Creative Soups & Salads

1 lemon
2 oranges
2 Golden Delicious apples, unpeeled
3 cups cubed cooked chicken
1/2 cup thinly sliced celery
3/4 cup mayonnaise

2 ozs. Grand Marnier or other
   orange-flavored liqueur
2 oranges, cut in half, fruit removed
2 ozs. toasted slivered almonds
8 butter lettuce leaves
black olives and watercress

With vegetable peeler, zester or grater, remove peel from the lemon and 2 oranges, being careful not to include any of the white pith. Finely chop peel. Cut oranges into sections. Drain off juice and set aside. Squeeze lemon. Combine lemon juice with orange juice. Core and dice apples. In a large glass or stainless steel bowl, combine chicken, celery, apples and peel. Stir in juice mixture. Refrigerate at least one hour. Mix mayonnaise and Grand Marnier. Fold into chicken mixture. Spoon chicken salad into hollowed-out orange shells. Arrange lettuce leaves on 4 individual plates. Place shells in lettuce cups, allowing 1 shell per serving. Sprinkle tops with toasted almonds. Garnish with black olives, reserved orange segments and a sprig of watercress. Makes 4 main dish servings.

Belgian Endive Salad

From Creative Soups & Salads

Serve this pretty, piquant salad with baked salmon, roast leg of lamb or chicken.

Orange Dressing, see below
1 head romaine
2 heads Belgian endive

1 small red onion
1 jar (6 ozs.) marinated artichoke hearts
2 oranges, thinly sliced

Prepare dressing and set aside. Tear romaine into bite-size pieces. Separate endive leaves. Slice onion and separate into rings. Cut artichoke hearts in half. Combine romaine, endive, onion rings, artichokes, and orange slices in a large salad bowl. Pour dressing over salad ingredients and toss lightly. Makes 4 to 6 servings.

Orange Dressing—Blend together 6 tablespoons olive oil, 3 tablespoons orange juice, 1-1/2 tablespoons lemon juice, 1 teaspoon grated orange peel, 1/4 teaspoon garlic salt and 1/8 teaspoon dry mustard.

Caesar Salad

From Creative Soups & Salads

Here's a salad that is fun to mix at the table in front of family or guests.

1 clove garlic, peeled
6 T. olive oil
3 T. lemon juice
1/2 tsp. salt
1/2 tsp. Worcestershire
1/2 tsp. Dijon-style mustard

freshly grated pepper
1/2 cup freshly grated Parmesan
8 anchovy fillets, chopped (if desired)
1 qt. torn romaine
1 raw egg
1-1/2 cups croutons

Rub cut clove of garlic around inside of the salad bowl. Mix together oil, lemon juice, salt, Worcestershire, mustard, pepper and half the cheese. Add anchovies and romaine. Toss lightly. Break egg onto salad and mix until blended. Sprinkle croutons and remaining cheese over salad. Makes 4 servings.

Peachy Chicken Salad

From Healthy Cooking On The Run

A colorful, crunchy salad that looks pretty, tastes good and offers nutrition plus. For a cool, light, summer supper or a refreshing luncheon, serve with soup, muffins and a light dessert.

1 cup cooked brown rice
2 cups diced cooked chicken
1/2 cup each celery and green pepper, coarsely chopped
1-1/2 cups cubed fresh or canned peaches, drained
1/4 cup chopped walnuts or almonds
1/4 cup mayonnaise
1 T. chopped onion
1-1/2 tsp. curry powder
1 T. lemon juice

Lightly toss together the rice, chicken, celery, green pepper, peaches and nuts. Make dressing of mayonnaise, onion, curry and lemon juice. Stir dressing into mixture. Chill thoroughly. Serve in lettuce cups. Garnish with toasted walnuts or almonds. 4-6 servings.

Layered Vegetable Salad

From Creative Soups & Salads
This vegetable quartet takes on the flavor-packed dressing as it chills.

1 lb. green beans, cooked and cut in 1/2-inch pieces
3 medium carrots, cooked and cut in 1/2-inch pieces
1 pkg. (10 ozs.) frozen peas, cooked or 1-1/4 cups fresh peas, cooked
2 medium beets, cooked, peeled and cut into 1/2-inch cubes
Horseradish Cream Dressing, page 135
2 T. minced fresh parsley

Arrange vegetables in attractive layers in a glass salad bowl. Pour dressing over the vegetables. Cover and refrigerate 1 hour. Garnish with parsley before serving. Makes 4 servings.

Horseradish Cream Dressing

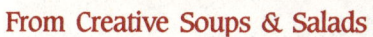

From Creative Soups & Salads

This dressing is excellent served on the Vegetable Salad, page 134. It also makes a good sauce for roast beef or corned beef.

1 large egg yolk
3 T. salad oil
1 T. fresh lemon juice
2 tsp. Dijon-style mustard
1 tsp. prepared horseradish
1/2 tsp. salt
1/4 tsp. white pepper
2 T. olive oil
1/4 cup sour cream

Insert the metal blade into food processor bowl. Add egg yolk, 1 tablespoon salad oil, lemon juice, mustard, horseradish, salt, and pepper. Process to mix. With machine running, gradually add the remaining salad oil and the olive oil. Add sour cream and process just until mixed. Makes approximately 3/4 cup.

Mexican Beef and Orange Salad

From Creative Soups & Salads

Peppers and oranges enliven this meat salad for a festive summer supper entree.

1-1/2 lbs. rare roast beef or steak
2 navel oranges
1 sweet red onion
1 green pepper, seeded
1/3 cup olive oil
1-1/2 T. white wine vinegar

1-1/2 T. lime or lemon juice
1/2 tsp. salt
1/2 tsp. ground cumin or Mexican seasoning
salad greens
fresh or canned red peppers
1 bunch cilantro (Chinese parsley)

Cut meat into strips. Peel and thinly slice oranges and onion. Slice pepper into strips. Place in a bowl. Mix together oil, vinegar, lime juice, salt and cumin. Pour over meat mixture. Cover and chill at least 2 hours. To serve, arrange greens on a platter. Spoon salad mixture onto greens. Garnish with red peppers and cilantro sprigs. Makes 6 main dish servings.

Note: If desired, cut red peppers, beginning at their tips almost to the stem end, making 5 or 6 strips to resemble flower petals.

Citrus Seafood Salad

From Favorite Seafood Recipes

Any firm white fish, local to your area, may be used in this recipe. Shrimp is also delicious prepared this way.

2 cups fresh fish fillets,
   or 2 cups cooked and cleaned shrimp
2 grapefruits, peeled, cored and sectioned
2 oranges, peeled, cored and sectioned
1/4 cup chopped green onions, with tops
salad greens
1/2 ripe avocado, peeled and sliced

Salad Dressing:
1/4 cup each vinegar, oil and catsup
2 T. sugar
1 tsp. chili powder
1 clove garlic, mashed

Poach fish in simmering, salted water for 8 to 10 minutes. Cool in liquid. When cold, remove from liquid and debone. Chill. Mix together grapefruit and orange sections. Add onion. Chill. Combine all ingredients for salad dressing. Just before serving, combine fish with fruit mixture. Moisten with salad dressing. Arrange greens on plates. Scoop salad onto greens. Garnish with avocado slices. Makes 4 servings.

Mountainous Noodles

From Wok Appetizers & Light Snacks

1 lb. thin fresh noodles
cooking oil
4 T. sesame oil
1/4 cup crunchy peanut butter
1 clove garlic, mashed

1/4 cup light soy sauce
1 T. Tabasco sauce
1/2 cup malt vinegar
1 T. Worcestershire sauce

Cook noodles in plenty of boiling water, adding 1 tablespoon cooking oil for each 2 quarts of water. When noodles are done, drain, rinse with tap water and drain well. Heat 2 tablespoons of the sesame oil and mix into drained noodles. Chill at least 1 hour. Blend remaining sesame oil and peanut butter into a paste. Add garlic, soy sauce, Tabasco, vinegar and Worcestershire sauce. Stir until well blended. Mound chilled noodles neatly on a platter and serve the sauce in a separate bowl. Allow guests to combine noodles and sauce to suit their own tastes. 6 to 8 servings.

Mountainous Noodles as a Centerpiece

From Wok Appetizers & Light Snacks
This is an attractive dish for a buffet luncheon. Mountainous Noodles are surrounded by garnishes and the sauce is served separately in a small bowl.

Mountainous Noodles, page 138
vegetable oil
1 egg, beaten
1 bunch cilantro, leaves only

1 cup bean sprouts
1/2 cup cooked, shredded chicken breast
1/2 cup cooked ham strips
8 red radish roses

Prepare noodles and sauce as directed in recipe. Chill until needed. Place a large skillet over medium-high heat. Sprinkle a few drops of oil into skillet. Use a paper towel to distribute oil evenly. Pour beaten egg into skillet. Cook without stirring until done. Remove from skillet and cut into 1/3 x 2-inch strips. Pile noodles neatly on a platter. Surround with garnishes, starting from the outer edge of the platter in the following order: cilantro leaves, bean sprouts, egg strips, shredded chicken and ham strips. Garnish with radish roses. Serve sauce in separate bowl. 6 to 8 servings.

Best of Muffins, Breads and etc.

Caramel Cinnamon Twists

From Bread Baking
Caramelized cinnamon-sugar gilds these spiral rolls with crunchy candy.

1 cup butter, melted
1 cup sour cream
1 tsp. salt
1 tsp. vanilla
1 pkg. active dry yeast
2 egg yolks
1 egg
3-1/2 cups all-purpose flour
1-1/2 cups sugar
2 tsp. cinnamon

Mix together hot butter, sour cream, salt and vanilla. The mixture should be lukewarm. Sprinkle in yeast. Beat egg yolks and egg until blended. Stir into yeast mixture. Stir in enough

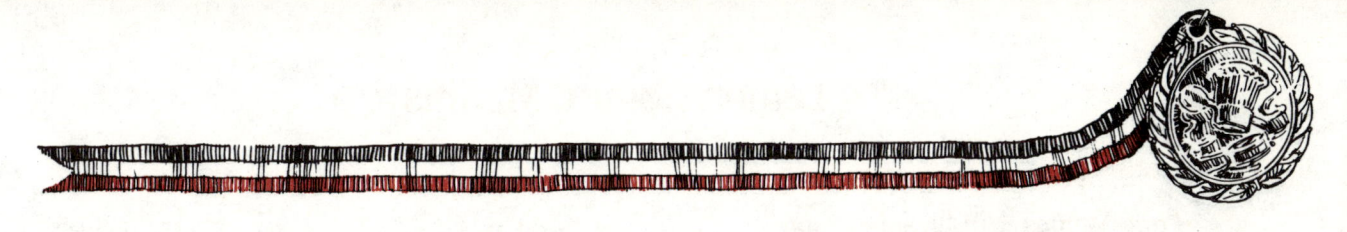

flour to make a soft dough. Beat until smooth. It is not necessary to knead this dough. Cover bowl with plastic wrap. Chill 2 hours. Mix sugar and cinnamon. Spread half of it on a board. Divide dough in half. Roll each piece of dough into a rectangle (15 x 18 inches). Turn dough in the cinnamon-sugar mixture so both sides are coated. Fold over three times, as you would fold a letter. Repeat rolling, coating and folding three times until sugar mixture is almost used. Roll into a rectangle 1/4 inch thick. Cut into strips 1/2 inch wide by 4 inches long. Twist strips. Dip in remaining cinnamon-sugar mixture. Lay on a greased baking sheet. Repeat with remaining dough and sugar mixture. Cover with towel. Let rise in a warm place until light and puffy. Bake in 375°F. oven 15 minutes, or until golden brown. Serve hot or reheat. Makes about 4 dozen twists.

Lemon Yogurt Muffins

From Muffins, Nut Breads & More

Lemon yogurt is our choice for this moist muffin. Be inventive and substitute your favorite yogurt flavor.

2 cups all-purpose flour
2-1/2 tsp. baking powder
1/2 tsp. each baking soda and salt
1 T. grated lemon peel
1 egg
1/4 cup oil
1/3 cup honey
1 carton (8 oz.) lemon yogurt

Preheat oven to 400°F. Stir together flour, baking powder, baking soda, salt and grated lemon peel. Mix egg, oil, honey and yogurt together well. Add this mixture to dry ingredients. Stir until just moistened. Fill greased or paper-lined muffin pans 2/3 full. Bake for 18 minutes, or until golden brown. Makes 12 muffins.

Banana Oatmeal Muffins

From Muffins, Nut Breads & More

Wake up your family with the mouth-watering aroma of these healthful breakfast muffins. Children are particularly fond of them.

1-1/2 cups all-purpose flour
1 cup quick-cooking oats
2 tsp. baking powder
1 tsp. baking soda
1/2 tsp. salt
1 egg

1/2 cup milk when using honey
 (3/4 cup milk when using sugar)
1/3 cup oil
1/2 cup honey or sugar
2/3 cup mashed banana

Preheat oven to 400°F. Stir together flour, oats, baking powder, baking soda and salt. Mix egg, milk, oil, honey or sugar and mashed banana together well. Add this mixture to dry ingredients. Stir until just moistened. Fill greased or paper-lined muffin pans 2/3 full. Bake for 20 minutes, or until golden brown. Makes about 16 muffins.

Panettone

From Bread Baking

Chewy raisins and nuts jewel this sweet brioche-style Italian bread.

3/4 cup milk
1 pkg. active dry yeast
1/4 cup lukewarm water
1/2 cup butter
1/2 cup sugar
3 eggs
3-1/2 cups all-purpose flour
1 tsp. each vanilla and grated lemon peel
1/2 tsp. cinnamon
1/2 cup each golden and dark raisins, plumped in brandy or dry sherry
1/2 cup slivered almonds or pine nuts
1 egg white, lightly beaten

Heat milk until warm. Sprinkle yeast into warm water and let stand until dissolved. Beat

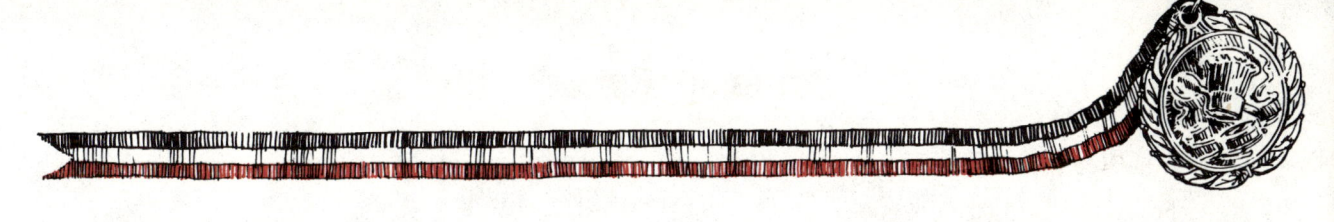

butter until creamy. Beat in sugar. Add eggs one at a time. Beat until smooth. Add 1 cup flour. Beat well. Stir in yeast, milk, vanilla, lemon peel and cinnamon. Gradually add remaining flour. Beat until smooth. Mix in raisins and almonds. Turn out on a lightly floured board and knead until smooth and no longer sticky. Place in a greased bowl. Butter top of dough lightly. Cover with a clean kitchen towel and let rise in a warm place until doubled in size. Turn out onto a floured board and knead lightly. Divide in half. Shape into two round cakes about 6 inches in diameter. Place on a greased baking sheet or in greased cake pans. Cover and let rise until doubled in size. Bake in 350°F. oven 30 minutes, or until golden brown. Let cool on a cake rack. Slice and serve warm or at room temperature. Makes 2 round loaves.

Pumpkin Raisin Muffins

From The Brunch Cookbook

If you like, sprinkle the tops of these muffins with the Crunchy Nut Topping.

1 egg
1/2 cup milk
1/2 cup canned pumpkin
1/4 cup melted butter
1/2 cup sugar
1-1/2 cups all-purpose flour
2 tsp. baking powder

1/2 tsp. salt
1/2 tsp. each cinnamon and nutmeg
1/2 cup raisins
Nut Crunch Topping (optional):
1/3 cup firmly packed brown sugar
1/3 cup chopped walnuts
1/2 tsp. cinnamon

Combine egg, milk, pumpkin, butter and sugar in a medium-sized bowl. Stir until blended. Sift flour, baking powder, salt and 1/2 teaspoon each of cinnamon and nutmeg into pumpkin mixture. Stir until just moistened. Batter should be lumpy. Fold in raisins. Fill greased muffin cups about two thirds full. Combine Nut Crunch Topping ingredients in a small bowl. Sprinkle evenly over tops of muffins. Bake at 400°F. for 18 to 20 minutes. Serve hot. Makes 12 muffins.

Blueberry Ginger Muffins

From Muffins, Nut Breads & More
Try this delicious and unusual combination.

2-1/2 cups all-purpose flour
1 T. baking powder
1/2 tsp. baking soda
1/2 tsp. salt
1/3 cup sugar
1 tsp. cinnamon
1/2 tsp. ginger

1 egg
1 cup buttermilk
1/4 cup oil
1/2 cup dark molasses
1 cup blueberries (rinsed and drained
    if they are canned or frozen)

Preheat oven to 400°F. Stir together flour, baking powder, baking soda, salt, sugar, cinnamon and ginger. Mix egg, buttermilk, oil and molasses together well. Add this mixture to dry ingredients. Stir until just moistened. Gently fold in blueberries. Fill greased or paper-lined muffin pans 2/3 full. Bake for 20 minutes, or until done. Makes 18 muffins.

Gingerbread

From Muffins, Nut Breads & More
Simply heavenly served warm with its own special buttermilk glaze.

1/2 cup butter or margarine
1/2 cup dark molasses
1/4 cup honey or sugar
1 egg
1 tsp. vanilla
1 cup whole wheat flour
1 cup unbleached all-purpose flour } or 2 cups all-purpose flour
2 tsp. baking powder
1-1/2 tsp. baking soda
1/2 tsp. salt
1 tsp. each ground ginger and cinnamon
1/4 tsp. each nutmeg and ground cloves
1/2 cup buttermilk

Preheat oven to 350°F. Cream butter. Mix in molasses, honey, egg and vanilla. Combine

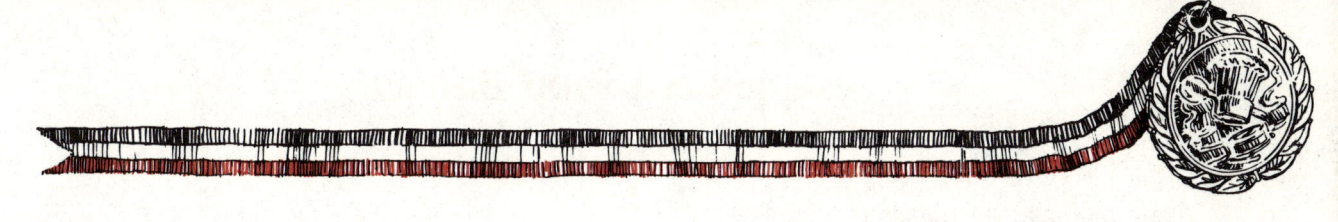

dry ingredients. Stir into butter mixture alternately with buttermilk. Pour batter into a greased and floured baking pan (9x9x2 inches). Bake 40 minutes or until done. Serve warm with Buttermilk Glaze.

BUTTERMILK GLAZE
3 T. butter or margarine
3 T. honey or sugar
1/4 cup buttermilk
1/4 tsp. baking soda
1/2 tsp. vanilla

Combine ingredients in a small saucepan. Cook over low heat until syrupy, about 15 minutes, stirring frequently. Spoon over hot gingerbread and serve.

Sesame Seed Drop Biscuits

From Muffins, Nut Breads & More

A blend of natural ingredients creates this wholesome biscuit.

1-1/2 cups whole wheat flour
1/2 cup wheat germ
1 T. baking powder
1/2 tsp. baking soda
1/2 tsp. salt
1/3 cup butter or margarine

1 egg
1 cup buttermilk
1 T. honey or sugar
1/4 cup melted butter or margarine
1/2 cup sesame seeds

Preheat oven to 400°F. Mix flour, wheat germ, baking powder, baking soda and salt together. Cut in butter until mixture resembles coarse cornmeal. Combine egg, buttermilk and honey. Stir this mixture into dry ingredients. Drop by tablespoonfuls onto a greased baking sheet. Brush with melted butter and sprinkle with sesame seeds. Bake 12 to 15 minutes. Makes 20 biscuits.

Danish Coffee Twist

From Bread Baking

The simple way in which this buttery yeast bread is cut and shaped results in its handsome pinwheel design. You have a choice of three fillings.

1 pkg. active dry yeast
1/4 cup warm water
1/2 cup butter
6 T. sugar
1/2 tsp. salt
1/2 tsp. cardamom **or** 1 tsp. grated orange peel **or** 2 tsp. vanilla
3 eggs
4 cups all-purpose flour
3/4 cup warm milk
Caramel, Nut or Chocolate Filling, page 155
1 egg white, beaten until frothy
pecan halves, chopped filberts or slivered almonds

continued

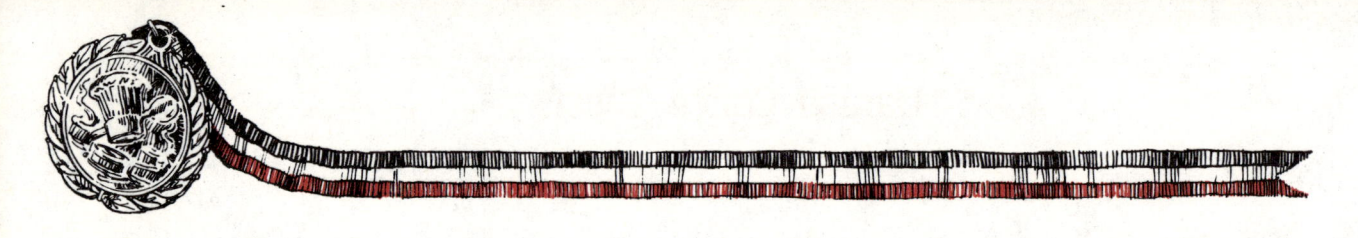

Sprinkle yeast into warm water and let stand until dissolved. Beat butter until creamy. Beat in sugar, salt, flavoring and eggs. Add 1 cup flour and beat well. Add warm milk and dissolved yeast. Beat until smooth. Gradually add remaining flour. Beat until smooth. Cover and let rise until doubled, about 1-1/2 hours. Turn out onto a floured board and knead lightly. Cut dough in half. Roll one half into a 10 x 14 inch rectangle. Spread with choice of filling. Roll up and place seam side down on a buttered baking sheet. Repeat with remaining dough and filling. Cut through rolls to within 1/2 inch of the bottom at 3/4 inch intervals. Pull and twist each slice to lay flat. Lay them first to one side and then the other. Cover with a towel and let rise in a warm place until doubled in size, about 45 minutes. Brush loaves with egg white and sprinkle with sugar and nuts. Bake in 325°F. oven 30 to 35 minutes, or until golden brown. Let cool on cake racks. Serve warm, cut in 1-inch slices.

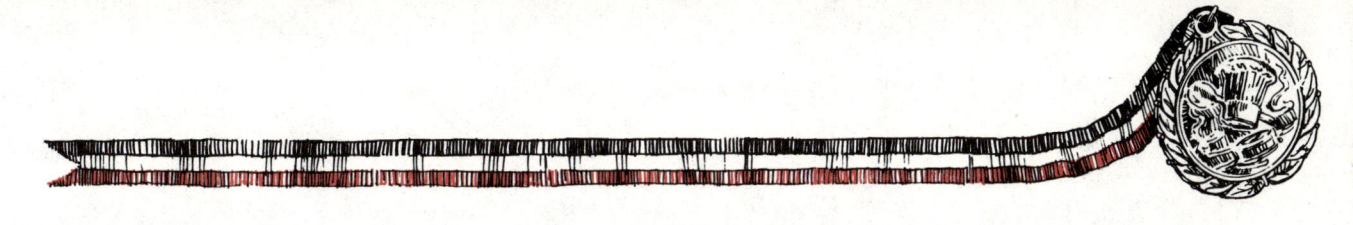

Caramel Pecan Filling: Spread each rectangle with 2 tablespoons butter. Sprinkle each with 1/2 cup firmly packed brown sugar and 1/4 cup chopped pecans. Roll. Proceed as directed.

Nut Streusel Filling: Mix together 1 can (8 oz.) almond paste, 1/4 cup soft butter, 2 tablespoons sugar, 1/3 cup finely chopped filberts, almonds or pecans and 1 egg. Beat until smooth. Spread half of mixture on each rectangle. Roll up. Proceed as directed.

Chocolate Streusel Filling: Mix 1/2 cup sugar, 1/4 cup all-purpose flour, 2 tablespoons butter, 1-1/2 teaspoons unsweetened ground cocoa and 1/2 teaspoon cinnamon until crumbly. Spread half of mixture on each rectangle. Roll up. Proceed as directed.

Peanut Butter Banana Bread

From Muffins, Nut Breads & More

Chopped peanuts add extra nutrition to this bread. A slice will boost your energy any time of day.

1/2 cup crunchy peanut butter
1/4 cup oil
1/2 cup honey
1 egg
1 cup mashed banana
2 cups whole wheat flour

1 cup wheat germ
1 T. baking powder
1/2 tsp. salt
1/2 cup chopped peanuts (optional)
3/4 cup milk

Preheat oven to 350°F. Mix peanut butter, oil, honey, egg and mashed banana together well. Combine flour, wheat germ, baking powder, salt and peanuts. Add dry ingredients to peanut butter mixture alternately with milk. Spread batter in a greased and floured loaf pan (9x5x3 inches). Bake for 1 hour, or until bread tests done. Cool in pan for about 5 minutes, then turn out on a wire rack. Makes 1 loaf.

Honey Walnut Bread

From Muffins, Nut Breads & More

1/4 cup butter or margarine
1 cup honey
1 egg
1 cup milk
1-1/4 cups whole wheat flour
1-1/4 cups unbleached all-purpose flour } or 2-1/2 cups all-purpose flour
1-1/2 tsp. baking soda
1/2 tsp. salt
1 cup walnuts, coarsely chopped

Preheat oven to 350°F. Cream butter, adding honey in a fine stream. Beat in egg and milk. Combine dry ingredients. Add to creamed ingredients, mixing well. Stir in nuts. Pour batter into a greased and floured loaf pan (9x5x3 inches). Garnish the top with walnut halves if desired. Bake for 1 hour and 10 minutes or until bread tests done. Cool in the pan for about 5 minutes, then turn out on a wire rack to cool. Makes 1 loaf.

Almond Danish

From The Brunch Cookbook

These richly flaked pastries, filled with delicate almond butter cream, literally melt in your mouth.

1 cup ice-cold butter,
    cut into 1-inch cubes
3 cups all-purpose flour
2 pkgs. active dry yeast
1/4 cup warm water
1/4 cup plus 1 tsp. sugar
1/2 cup evaporated milk
2 eggs, room temperature
1 tsp. salt
paper cupcake liners

Butter Cream:
3/4 cup butter
1-1/4 cups powdered sugar
1/4 cup almond paste
2 tsp. vanilla

Almond Icing:
1 cup powdered sugar
2 T. milk
1/2 tsp. almond extract

Place butter and flour in large mixing bowl or work bowl of a food processor. Process or beat butter and flour together until butter is the size of kidney beans, no smaller. Refrigerate

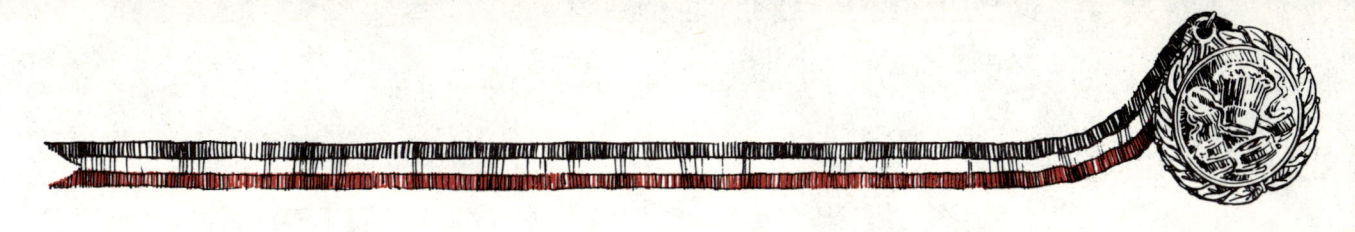

mixture while preparing yeast mixture. Combine yeast, water and 1 tsp. sugar. Stir gently. Cover and let sit for 10 minutes in a warm oven to "proof" yeast. Add remaining sugar, evaporated milk, eggs and salt. Stir to blend. Pour this mixture over the butter and flour mixture, stir together until just blended. You should still have lumps of butter throughout. Cover and refrigerate dough for 4 hours or overnight.

To assemble pastries: Mix Butter Cream ingredients in a bowl until smooth and creamy. Set aside. Remove dough from refrigerator and divide in half. Return one half to the refrigerator. Roll remaining portion on a lightly floured surface into a 8 x 16-inch rectangle. Spread evenly with one half of Butter Cream. Roll up from the long side. Cut roll into sixteen 1-inch wide slices. Repeat with remaining dough and Butter Cream. Place each slice in a cupcake liner. Place pastries 1 inch apart on a baking sheet. Cover pastries and rise in warm place until doubled in volume, about 1 hour. Bake at 400°F. for 12 to 15 minutes, or until light golden brown. Prepare Almond Icing by mixing all ingredients together in a small bowl. While pastries are still warm, drizzle with the icing. Makes 32 pastries.

Best of Desserts

Crepes Melba

From Crepes & Omelets

A peaches and cream filling covered with raspberry sauce.

8 Dessert Crepes, page 165
1/2 cup whipping cream
1/4 cup sugar
1/2 cup ricotta cheese
1 cup fresh raspberries
1/4 cup sugar
2 T. Triple Sec, Kirsch, or orange juice
2 to 3 fresh peaches, peeled and sliced

Make crepes as directed. Set aside. Whip cream until soft peaks form. Stir in 1/4 cup sugar and beat until stiff. Fold whipped cream into ricotta cheese. Puree fresh raspberries in blender. Strain to remove seeds. Add 1/4 cup sugar and Triple Sec. Heat sauce just before serving. When ready to fill crepes add peaches to cheese mixture and spoon into crepes. Place filled crepes on serving dishes. Spoon warm Raspberry Sauce, page 164, over the crepes. Makes 4 servings.

Beignets

From Crepes & Omelets
Cooked crepes cut into ribbons and fried. Serve hot with Chocolate Rum Sauce or Raspberry Sauce, page 164.

1 egg
2 T. oil
1-1/4 cups milk
1 T. brandy

1 cup all-purpose flour
1/2 tsp. salt
1/2 tsp. cinnamon
1 T. sugar

Place egg, oil, milk, brandy, flour and salt in blender or food processor container. Blend on high speed 20 to 30 seconds. Scrape down sides of container. Blend a few more seconds. Cook crepes in large 10-inch pan, according to directions on page 77. Cut crepes into 1-inch strips. Heat approximately 1 inch of oil to 375°F. in large frying pan or electric skillet. Drop in crepe strips. The strips should stay fairly flat while they are cooking. Turn them over once or twice and remove when they are a nice golden color. Drain for a minute or two on paper toweling. Sprinkle with sugar and cinnamon which have been mixed together. Serve hot. Makes 4 servings.

Sauces for Crepes

Raspberry Sauce:
1 pkg. (10 ozs.) frozen raspberries, defrosted
1 T. Triple Sec or Kirsch

1 tsp. lemon juice

Place berries and syrup in blender container. Cover and puree. Strain through sieve to remove seeds. Stir in liqueur and lemon juice. Makes 1 cup. Good over crepes, or folded into whipped or sour cream for a filling.

Chocolate Rum Sauce:
1 can (5.5 ozs.) Hershey's Chocolate Syrup
1 tsp. vanilla

1-1/2 T. dark rum
2 T. heavy cream

Combine ingredients in small saucepan. Stir until blended. Heat but do not boil. Makes about 3/4 cup sauce.

Classic Dessert Crepes

From Crepes & Omelets

There's no end to the ways dessert crepes can be used. Keep a supply in the freezer!

2 eggs
2 T. melted butter
1-1/4 cups milk
2 T. brandy or orange liqueur
1 T. sugar
1 cup sifted cake flour
1/2 tsp. salt

Place ingredients in blender or food processor container in the order listed. Blend at high speed 20 to 30 seconds. Scrape down sides of the container. Blend a few more seconds. Cook according to directions given on page 77. Makes 16 to 20 5-inch crepes.

Butterscotch Squares

From Fast & Delicious

This is a delicious and easy dessert. Not many guess the mystery ingredient – zucchini. The recipe can easily be doubled.

1/3 cup butter or margarine
1 T. hot water
1 cup firmly packed brown sugar
1 egg
1 tsp. vanilla
1 cup all-purpose flour (unsifted)

1 tsp. baking powder
1/8 tsp. baking soda
1/2 tsp. salt
3/4 cup peeled, diced zucchini
1/2 cup chopped walnuts
1/3 cup butterscotch chips

In saucepan over medium heat, melt margarine with hot water. Place in a mixing bowl. Add sugar and beat well with a fork. Cool. Add egg and vanilla; beat again. In a separate bowl, mix dry ingredients together. Add to sugar mixture. Stir until just blended. Stir in zucchini and nuts. Pour mixture into a buttered and floured 9 x 9-inch pan. Sprinkle with butterscotch chips. Bake for 25 minutes at 350°F. Cool in pan. Cut into squares. Serves 6.

Raisin Rice Pudding

From Easy Microwave Cooking

Stir up this pudding, and stir up some old-fashioned memories. Perfect for leftover rice.

2 eggs, slightly beaten
1 pkg. (3 ozs.) instant vanilla pudding
2 cups milk
1-1/2 cups rice, cooked
1/2 tsp. vanilla
1/2 cup raisins

In a glass bowl or 2-1/2 quart Corningware casserole, mix pudding into beaten eggs. Stir in remaining ingredients. Microwave 7 minutes, stirring every two minutes. Cool or chill before serving. Makes 6 servings.

Pappy's Special Angel Torte

From Easy Microwave Cooking

Light and rich in one bite, this dessert is a favorite for bridge club or party dinners. Make it the day before.

1 envelope unflavored gelatin
1/2 cup cold milk
3 egg yolks, slightly beaten
1-1/2 cups milk
1 cup sugar

1 small angel food cake
3 egg whites, stiffly beaten
1 cup (1/2 pt.) cream, whipped
1/2 tsp. vanilla
Caramel Sauce, page 169

Sprinkle gelatin over 1/2 cup milk to soften. Mix yolks, 1-1/2 cups milk and sugar in a 4-cup glass measure or bowl. Microwave 4 to 5 minutes just until boiling, stirring often after the first two minutes. Add softened gelatin. Cool. Break angel food into pieces (remove crust if desired). Lightly fill a loaf pan or pretty serving casserole with cake pieces. When custard is cool, fold beaten egg whites and cream together. Then fold in custard and vanilla. Pour this mixture over pieces of cake, working it into the spaces. Refrigerate overnight. Serve with Caramel Sauce. Makes 12 servings.

Caramel Sauce

From Easy Microwave Cooking
Great over ice cream and for Pappy's Special Angel Torte on page 168!

5 T. butter
1 cup brown sugar
1/4 cup milk, evaporated milk, or cream*
1/2 tsp. vanilla
2 T. white corn syrup

Combine ingredients in a 2 or 4-cup glass measure. Microwave 2 minutes on medium (50%) power. Stir hard to blend. This sauce thickens as it cools. Reheat 30 to 45 seconds. Avoid overheating as it will cause the sauce to sugar. Makes 1 cup.

*When making this sauce for Pappy's Dessert, page 168, you can ''borrow'' 1/4 cup whipping cream from the dessert ingredients, decreasing the amount of cream used in Pappy's Dessert to 3/4 cup.

To help make timing less critical and prevent sugar crystals from forming in sweet sauces, add 2 tablespoons white corn syrup for each cup of sugar used.

Chocolate Peanut Bars

From Favorite Cookie Recipes

1 cup butter, at room temperature
1/2 cup granulated sugar
1-1/2 cups firmly packed brown sugar
2 eggs, separated at room temperature
1 tsp. vanilla
2 cups all-purpose flour

1 tsp. baking powder
1/4 tsp. baking soda
1/4 tsp. salt
1 pkg. (6 ozs.) semi-sweet chocolate chips
1 cup Spanish peanuts

Beat butter, granulated sugar and 1/2 cup of the brown sugar together until creamy. Beat in egg yolks and vanilla. In a separate bowl, stir together flour, baking powder, soda and salt. Add to creamed mixture. Beat well. Pat out dough into a greased 10 x 15-inch baking pan. Sprinkle with chocolate chips, pressing in gently. Beat egg whites until soft peaks form. Beat in remaining 1 cup brown sugar. Continue beating until stiff. Spread meringue mixture over top of chocolate chips. Sprinkle with peanuts. Bake in a 350°F. oven for 20 to 25 minutes, or until set and golden brown. Let cool, then cut into bars. Makes about 5 dozen.

Hints: If using food processor, DON'T make meringue in it. Use electric beaters or wire whisk.

Lemon Loaf Cake

From Food Processor Cookbook

A tender, delicate pound-type cake that can be thinly sliced to serve with tea or to accompany fresh fruit or berries for a delightful dessert.

2 cups cake flour (sift before measuring)
1/4 tsp. baking powder
1/4 tsp. salt
1-1/2 cups sugar
1/2 cup (1 cube) butter, cut in 5 or 6 pieces
3 large eggs
1/2 cup sour cream
zest of 1 lemon, finely grated
1 to 2 tsp. lemon extract

Grease the ends of an 8-1/2 x 4-1/2, or a 9 x 3-3/4 or two 4-1/2 x 3-inch loaf pans. Line sides and bottom with waxed paper or baking parchment. Preheat oven to 325°F. Insert steel

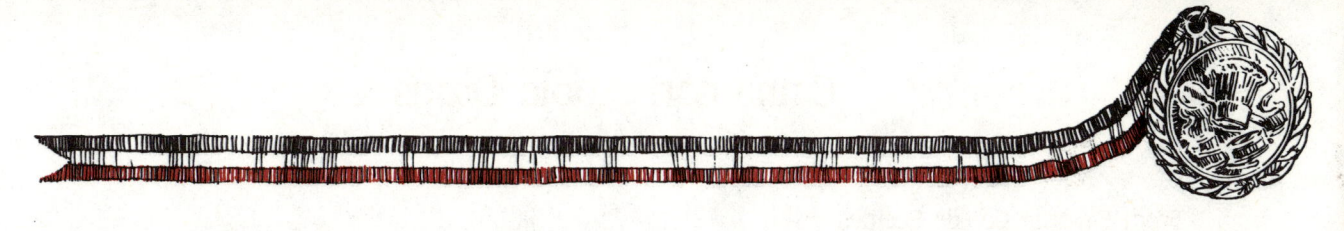

blade into food processor bowl. Add flour, baking powder, salt, sugar, and butter. Process with 5 or 6 "on-off" turns until butter is blended into the other ingredients. Mixture will look somewhat like cornmeal. Remove processor cover and add eggs, sour cream, lemon zest and extract. Replace cover and process with about 8 "on-off" turns. Stop and scrape bowl. Cover and process 2 more "on-off" turns, or just until ingredients are mixed. Mixture will have a grainy appearance. Do not over-process. Turn batter into prepared pan or pans. Bake in the middle of preheated 325°F. oven 1 hour and 25 to 30 minutes for large cake or 1 hour and 10 to 15 minutes for small cakes, or until center of crack appears dry. Cake will have a deep brown top crust. If cake appears to be overbrowning, reduce temperature to 300°F. and bake until done. Do not underbake.

Cinnamon Apple Drops

From Favorite Cookie Recipes

This chewy cookie is packed full of healthy ingredients.

2/3 cup butter, at room temperature
1-1/4 cups firmly packed brown sugar
2 eggs
1/4 cup plain yogurt
1 cup each all-purpose flour
   and whole wheat flour
1 tsp. each baking powder and cinnamon

1/2 tsp. each salt, baking soda,
   and allspice
1-1/2 cups coarsely grated,
   peeled and seeded tart apple
1 cup raisins
3/4 cup chopped walnuts or pecans

Beat butter and sugar together until creamy. Beat in eggs and yogurt. In separate bowl, stir together flours, baking powder, cinnamon, salt, soda and allspice. Add to creamed mixture. By hand, stir in apples, raisins and nuts. Drop by tablespoonfuls onto lightly greased baking sheets. Bake in a 375°F. oven for 8 to 10 minutes, or until golden brown. Remove immediately to wire racks to cool. Makes 4 dozen.

Hints: If using food processor, shred peeled and seeded apple with shredder attachment first.
Remove from bowl. Prepare dough.

Oatmeal Chocolate Chippers

From Favorite Cookie Recipes

1 cup butter or margarine, at room temperature
3/4 cup each granulated sugar and firmly packed brown sugar
2 eggs
1 tsp. vanilla
3/4 cup each all-purpose flour and whole wheat flour
1 tsp. baking soda
1/2 tsp. salt
2 cups quick cooking rolled oats
1 cup chopped walnuts or pecans
1 large package (12 ozs.) chocolate chips

Beat butter and sugars together until creamy. Beat in eggs and vanilla. In a separate bowl, stir together flours, soda and salt. Add to creamed mixture. Beat well. By hand, stir in oats, nuts and chips. Drop by rounded teaspoonfuls onto greased baking sheets. Bake in a 350°F. oven for 10 to 12 minutes, or until golden brown. Remove to wire racks to cool. Makes about 6 dozen.

Hint: If using food processor, stir oats, nuts and chocolate chips in by hand.

Creamy Orange Fondue

From The Brunch Cookbook

This is delightful to serve when summer fruits are at their best. Plates of assorted fruits are lovely to look at, and leftovers can go into a nice salad. Dieters appreciate this dessert because they can just nibble on the fruits—if they can resist the fondue!

1/4 cup butter
1/4 cup all-purpose flour
1-1/2 cups half-and-half
1/4 cup sugar
zest of one orange, finely grated
1 pkg. (8 ozs.) cream cheese, cubed
1/2 cup Grand Marnier liqueur

For Dipping:

Fresh fruits—strawberries, cherries, green seedless grapes, apricots, bananas, pears, apples, peaches

Canned fruits—mandarin oranges, pineapple chunks

Cubes of pound cake—chocolate is especially nice

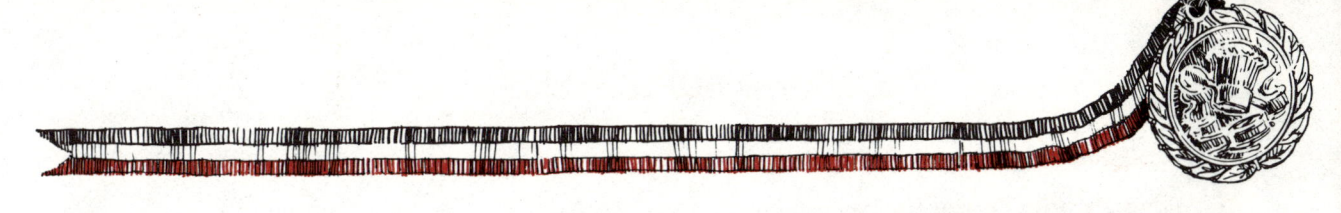

In a heavy-bottomed saucepan, melt butter over medium heat. Whisk in flour. Slowly add half-and-half, stirring till smooth. Add sugar and orange zest. Stir in cubed cream cheese until melted. Add Grand Marnier. Cook until mixture is just bubbly. Pour into a fondue pot and keep warm over a votive candle. Use an assortment of fresh fruits for dipping. Be sure to have plenty of napkins on hand, as well as individual dessert plates. Serves 8 to 10.

Kourabiedes

From Favorite Cookie Recipes

After they finish baking, these Greek butter cookies are meant to be completely buried in powdered sugar, like a great snowfall. They are a lovable holiday cookie, that can be shaped into rounds, crescents, S's and cut-outs.

1 cup butter, at room temperature
2 T. powdered sugar
1 egg yolk
1/2 cup blanched almonds,
    ground and lightly toasted

1/2 tsp. almond extract
2 cups all-purpose flour
about 2 cups powdered sugar

Beat butter and 2 tablespoons powdered sugar together until creamy. Mix in egg yolk, almonds and almond extract. Stir in flour until blended. Pinch off pieces of dough and roll into 3/4-inch balls. Flatten slightly and place on greased baking sheet. Bake in 325°F. oven for 20 to 25 minutes, or until very lightly browned on the edges. Let cool until lukewarm. Cover bottom of shallow pan with waxed paper. Sift powdered sugar in 1/8-inch thick layer over waxed paper. Transfer cookies onto it. Sift more sugar over top of cookies. When cool, transfer to an airtight container. Makes about 2-1/2 dozen.

Upside-Down Rhubarb Cake

From Fast & Delicious

1 T. butter
3 cups diced rhubarb
1-1/4 cups sugar
2 T. all-purpose flour
1 tsp. orange rind
1/2 tsp. cinnamon
1 cup all-purpose flour

2 T. sugar
2 tsp. baking powder
1/2 tsp. salt
1 egg
1/4 cup heavy cream
1/4 cup frozen orange juice,
    undiluted and thawed

Butter an 8-inch square baking pan with the 1 tablespoon of butter. Spread rhubarb in pan. Combine next four ingredients. Sprinkle over rhubarb. Make batter by combining the 1 cup of flour with remaining ingredients, except orange juice. If mixture seems too thick, add a little more cream. Spoon over rhubarb mixture. Bake at 350°F. for 25 minutes. Spread top with orange juice. Bake 15 minutes longer. Invert hot cake onto a cake plate. Serve with whipped cream, if desired.

Kentucky Butter Cake

From The Brunch Cookbook

If you like butter you'll love this cake. The hot butter sauce poured over the baked cake makes it exceptionally moist and delicious.

1 cup butter, at room temperature
2 cups sugar
4 eggs
1 cup buttermilk
2 tsp. vanilla
3 cups all-purpose flour
1 tsp. baking powder
1/2 tsp. baking soda
1/2 tsp. salt

Butter Sauce: 1 cup sugar
1/4 cup water
1/2 cup butter
1 T. vanilla

In a large mixing bowl, cream the butter and sugar with an electric mixer until fluffy. Beat eggs into the mixture one at a time, beating well after each addition. Stir in buttermilk and vanilla. Sift together flour, baking powder, baking soda and salt. Add to butter mixture, combining well. Pour into a buttered tube or bundt pan. Bake at 325°F. for 60 to 65 minutes, or until cake tests done. Make Butter Sauce. Combine sugar, water and butter in a small saucepan and cook, stirring constantly until mixture is smooth and hot. Do not boil. Remove from heat and stir in vanilla. Pierce the entire surface of the cake with a fork. Pour hot Butter Sauce over cake. Let cool. Serves 12.

Swedish Spritz

From Favorite Cookie Recipes

In Scandinavian homes, the buttery spritz is as integral to Christmas as the evergreen tree is to an American Christmas. And it is one that always stars on our holiday platter. Children delight in cranking out the dough with a cookie press.

1 cup butter, at room temperature
2/3 cup sugar
1 egg
1 tsp. vanilla
1/2 tsp. almond extract

2-1/2 cups all-purpose flour
1/2 tsp. baking powder
1/8 tsp. salt

Beat butter and sugar together until creamy. Mix in egg, vanilla and almond extract. In a separate bowl, stir together flour, baking powder and salt. Add to creamed mixture, mixing until smooth. Pack dough into a cookie tube press, using the thin flat wafer cut-out. Press out long strips of dough on greased baking sheets. Bake in a 350°F. oven for 8 to 10 minutes, or until edges of cookies are golden brown. Place cookie sheets on wire racks and with a sharp knife, cut diagonally across the strips making 2-1/2-inch cookies. Makes about 5 dozen.

Hint: Use any cookie press plate design desired.

Blueberry Cheesecake

From No Salt, No Sugar, No Fat Cookbook

1 pound cottage cheese
2 egg whites
1/2 cup plain low fat or nonfat yogurt
1 tsp. vanilla

2 tsp. lemon juice
1/4 cup frozen orange juice concentrate
2 ripe bananas, cut up
3 T. flour

Blend cheese, egg whites, yogurt, vanilla and lemon juice in a food processor blender. When ingredients are thoroughly mixed add fruit juice concentrate, bananas and flour. Continue blending until mixture is creamy. This takes 2 to 3 minutes in a food processor. Pour into a non-stick 9-inch pie pan and bake in pre-heated 350°F. oven for 45 minutes. Cool. Cover with topping.

TOPPING FOR CHEESECAKE

1 cup undrained crushed pineapple
1/4 cup frozen orange juice concentrate

1 T. cornstarch
1 cup fresh or frozen blueberries

Combine all ingredients in a small saucepan. Cook over medium heat stirring constantly until sauce thickens. Cool and pour sauce over pie. For a smoother sauce puree in blender. Makes 8 servings.

Swedish Almond Slices

From Favorite Cookie Recipes
These twice-baked cookies are perfect coffee dunkers.

1 cup butter, at room temperature	3 cups all-purpose flour
1 cup sugar	1 tsp. baking powder
2 eggs	1/4 tsp. baking soda
3 T. sour cream	1/8 tsp. salt
1/2 tsp. almond extract	2/3 cup slivered blanched almonds

Beat butter and sugar together until creamy. Add eggs, sour cream and almond extract. Beat until smooth. In a separate bowl, stir together flour, baking powder, soda and salt. Add to creamed mixture. Beat well. Mix in nuts. Turn out onto a greased baking sheet and pat into 3 strips, each about 2-1/2 inches wide and 1/2 inch high. Bake in a 350°F. oven for 25 to 30 minutes, or until golden brown. Remove from the oven and cut into 1/2 inch slices. Lay each slice flat on baking sheets and return to a 350°F. oven for 10 to 15 minutes, or until lightly browned. Remove to wire racks to cool. Makes about 4 dozen.

Chocolate Souffle

From Quiche & Souffle Cookbook

6 cup, well-buttered souffle dish	3 T. butter
3/4 cup milk	3 T. flour
2 ozs. bitter chocolate	5 egg yolks
7 T. sugar	7 egg whites

Preheat oven to 375°F. Sprinkle inside of buttered souffle dish with a little sugar. Heat milk, chocolate and 2 tablespoons sugar together in a small saucepan until chocolate is melted. Set aside. Melt butter in a medium-size saucepan. Remove from heat. Stir in flour and 4 tablespoons sugar. Gradually stir in chocolate-milk-sugar mixture. Return to heat. Stir until mixture thickens and resembles a chocolate cream sauce. Remove from heat. Very rapidly beat egg yolks into chocolate mixture. Transfer to a large bowl. Beat egg whites until stiff, but not dry. Add the remaining tablespoon of sugar. Beat 30 seconds. Fold into chocolate base. Pour into prepared souffle dish. Bake in preheated oven 20 minutes. Serve at once. 6 to 8 servings.

Index

Swedish Almond Slices 184
Peachy Chicken Salad 132
Peanut Butter Banana Bread 156
Pecan Spread 25
Pepper Steak With Cream 66
Pork
    Country Sausage 86
    Pork Chops in Orange Sauce 78
Pork Chops in Orange Sauce 78
Pot Roast Pacific 67
Pumpkin Raisin Muffins 148
Quiche a la Provencale 94
Raisin Rice Pudding 167
Rum Chicken 48
Salmon Mousse 96
San Francisco Cioppino 35
Sauces for Crepes 164
Sausage & Mushroom Streudel 102
Sausage Appetizers 16
Seafood Frittata 98

Seafood Gumbo a la Bundy 38
Sengalese Apple-Curry Soup 31
Sesame Seed Drop Biscuits 152
Sesame Shrimp 20
Seviche 22
Shanghai Meatballs 18
Skewered Shrimp, Avocado & Scallops 21
Sole Surprises 60
Soupe Au Pistou 30
Sour Cream Baked Chicken 50
Sour Cream Pancakes 100
Spinach Tart 110
Spring Bounty Soup 28
Stuffed Green Peppers Gallia Palace 118
Swedish Almond Slices 184
Swedish Spritz 182
Swordfish Stuffed With Lobster 58
Upside Down Rhubarb Cake 179
Vegetable Stew 82
Zucchini Puffs 115

190   Index

METRIC CONVERSION CHART

Liquid or Dry Measuring Cup (based on an 8 ounce cup)

1/4 cup = 60 ml
1/3 cup = 80 ml
1/2 cup = 125 ml
3/4 cup = 190 ml
1 cup = 250 ml
2 cups = 500 ml

Liquid or Dry Measuring Cup (based on a 10 ounce cup)

1/4 cup = 80 ml
1/3 cup = 100 ml
1/2 cup = 150 ml
3/4 cup = 230 ml
1 cup = 300 ml
2 cups = 600 ml

Liquid or Dry Teaspoon and Tablespoon

1/4 tsp. = 1.5 ml
1/2 tsp. = 3 ml
1 tsp. = 5 ml
3 tsp. = 1 tbs. = 15 ml

Temperatures

°F		°C
200	=	100
250	=	120
275	=	140
300	=	150
325	=	160
350	=	180
375	=	190
400	=	200
425	=	220
450	=	230
475	=	240
500	=	260
550	=	280

Pan Sizes (1 inch = 25 mm)

8-inch pan (round or square) = 200 mm x 200 mm
9-inch pan (round or square) = 225 mm x 225 mm
9 x 5 x 3-inch loaf pan = 225 mm x 125 mm x 75 mm
1/4 inch thickness = 5 mm
1/8 inch thickness = 2.5 mm

Pressure Cooker

100 Kpa = 15 pounds per square inch
70 Kpa = 10 pounds per square inch
35 Kpa = 5 pounds per square inch

Mass

1 ounce = 30 g
4 ounces = 1/4 pound = 125 g
8 ounces = 1/2 pound = 250 g
16 ounces = 1 pound = 500 g
2 pounds = 1 kg

Key (America uses an 8 ounce cup - Britain uses a 10 ounce cup)

ml = milliliter
l = liter
g = gram
K = Kilo (one thousand)
mm = millimeter
m = milli (a thousandth)
°F = degrees Fahrenheit

°C = degrees Celsius
tsp. = teaspoon
T. = tablespoon
Kpa = (pounds pressure per square inch)
This configuration is used for pressure cookers only.

Metric equivalents are rounded to conform to existing metric measuring utensils.